# The Little Business Book
## Five Steps to Your First Million

### Learning the Essentials:
### Sales, Customer Service,
### Operations, Finance, and Admin

From the Little Biz Series – *How to Grow a Successful Small Business*

**Dick Scoppettone**

*To Jiggs,*
*for being such a good boy*

And to all who roam the caverns of curiosity
and dreams, may your smallest venture
become your biggest success.


ISBN-13: 978-1515303473
ISBN-10: 1515303470


© 2015 Dick Scoppettone
Little Biz Books
111 Bean Creek Road, #146
Scotts Valley, CA 95066
dick@littlebiz.us

# TABLE OF CONTENTS

Introduction .................................................................................... iv

Step One – Administration ............................................................. 6
*Tracking Your Business Records 6 – Calendars and Scheduling 7 – Uniforms and Lockers 7 – Credit Cards 8 – Receptionist Duties 8 – Follow-up Calls 8 – Filing Systems 9 – Employee Records 9 – Billing Records 9 –Vendor Contacts 10 – Software 10 – Meetings and Agendas 12 – Office Equipment, Books, and Industry Publications 12 – Lease Agreement 13 – Memberships, Certifications, and Licenses 13 – Insurance 13 – Business Plan 14 – IRS 15 – Leadership 15 – IT Case Study 17 – Administration Highlights 19*

Step Two – Operations ................................................................ 20
*Hire Slowly, Fire Quickly 20 – Employee Handbook 21 – Full Time and Part Time Employees 21 – Job Descriptions 21 – Probationary Period, Sick Pay, Holidays 22 – Benefits, Insurance, Work Comp 23 – Performance Reviews 24 – Company Property 24 – Employee Conduct 24 – Wages and Overtime 24 – Health and Safety 25 – Termination 25 – Operations Manager 25 – Hiring Employees 26 – Firing Employees 27 – Safety Training 27 –Maintenance and Repair 28 –Licenses and Permits 28 – Employee Relations 28 – What's Good About Employees 28 – Optometrist Case Study 29 – Operations Highlights 32*

Step Three – Finance .................................................................. 33
*Pricing Goods and Services 33 – Typical Expenses 35 – Accounting Systems 36 – The P&L and Balance Sheet 36 –Sample Profit & Loss Statement 37 – Hiring a Bookkeeper 40 – How To Use The Numbers 40 – Sample Cash Flow Statement 42 – Forms of Payment 42 – Targeting Revenue Goals 43 – Budgeting 44 – Payroll 44 – Loans and Lenders 45 – Your Credit Score 45 – Average Income for Small Businesses 46 – Locksmith Case Study 47 – Finance Highlights 50*

Step Four – Marketing & Sales ................................................... 51
*The Difference Between Marketing and Sales 51 – The Top Forty Marketing Tools 53 – The Most Important Ingredients In The Sales Process 64 – Overview of Sales Elements 65 – Trust, Credibility, Relationship, Value 67 – How To Ask And Answer Your Customers' Questions 69 – What You Don't Do 70 – Selling Value Over Price 71 –The Sales Process In Depth 72 – Destination Resort Case Study 80 – Marketing & Sales Highlights 81*

Step Five – Customer Service ..................................................... 83
*It's Not About Price 83 – Value vs. Price 85 – Is This Really Customer Service? 86 – What Is Client-centered Service? 87 – New Ways To Market Value 89 – Objectives of Client-centered Service 89 – How to Give Client-centered Service 90 – Offer Them What*

*They Can't Get Elsewhere 91 – Let Your Competitors Have It 91 – The Value Test 92 – Sporting Goods Case Study 93 – Customer Service Highlights 95*

The Little Business Book Summary .......................................................97

Appendix – Case Studies.........................................................................99
*Contract Manufacturer 101 – HVAC 103 – Building Designer 105– Bakery 108– Civil and Structural Engineer 110 –Chiropractor 113 – Funeral & Cremation Service 115 – Hair Salon 117 – Building Contractor 119 – Small Business Service 121 –Landscaping 123 – Auto Repair 125 – SBA Lender 127 – Business Consultant 130 – Business Broker 134*

Glossary ....................................................................................................138
Bibliography ............................................................................................141
Acknowledgements.................................................................................142
About the Author ....................................................................................143
Future Books in the Little Biz Series ....................................................144

# INTRODUCTION

When my wife and I started our small business 15 years ago, I knew I was ready to be my own boss. I had been a travel agent for the preceding decade with a wonderfully loyal clientele. That was the best part of the job, but I discovered early on that vacationing customers could be quickly turned off when told they had just missed the 14-day advance purchase and their airfare would now cost five times as much.

As I listened to my fellow agents break the same bad news to clients time and again, I realized that this experience wasn't a good one for either our customers or my compadres. I knew that success was all about service, so I tried a different approach.

I imagined that the customer who just pulled into my parking lot already had the tilting palm trees of Kaanapali Beach on Maui in his head. He was already on vacation before he walked through my front door and I wasn't going to jolt him out of it with "I'm sorry, but that's not available." Instead, I decided I would mentally go on vacation with him, and together we'd be teeing off on the 18th hole at the Plantation golf course, energized by the fabulous views of Molokai and Lanai.

When you treat customers the way you want to be treated, it always works. When you let them know that all they have to do is Ring Bell for Service, they'll always come back and you'll be mucho successful.

I decided to go into business for myself, figuring I might as well pocket all the dough rather than work for peanuts. I could have started my own travel agency, something I knew a lot about. Instead, along with another couple, my wife and I started a business that she was good at, and while they appointed me CEO, it took me a half-dozen fiscal years to learn how to be really good at it.

This is the story of how that business worked and how, after 15 years, we finally made our first million in annual revenue. That's right, 1 million dollars, not 30 million, not 50 million. This book isn't about big. It's about the reality of what you and I face. Big corporations live in a world completely unrelated us. What you need to know is that there are only about a thousand big corporations in the U.S., but there are 29 and a half million of us small business owners. We don't put people on hold for 45 minutes, or demand exorbitant interest rates, or pound our customers with questionable advertising on TV. Our world is about small business and it's distinctly different from the way big businesses operate. This book is about you, not Walmart. So get off that fictional bus and join me for the most real ride of your life – running your own Little Biz.

Step One begins with Administration: how to keep your whole enterprise from falling apart before you even open the door. Step Two, Operations, shows you how to deal with employees. Profit and loss and how to get a loan is explained in Step Three. In Step Four, you'll learn the difference between Marketing and Sales. And Step Five opens with the most important ingredient in the Little Biz recipe for success – customer service, or what I call client-centered service. Running a prosperous small business isn't just about service – it's *all* about service. If you want to be the low-price leader toss this book and put up a sign that reads, "There's no value here. I'm just cheap." Only big business can give away the store. Why? Their most valued customers are stockholders, not point-of-purchase customers like you and I.

Interspersed within these five steps are case studies that will give you valuable words of wisdom from actual owners of 20 different small businesses.

As you follow these steps to your first million, you will be able to chart your progress toward building a successful company, one that will give you and your family the kind of opportunities that can only come from running your own small business.

Let's get you off to a good start with the first and most basic step: Administration.

**STEP ONE**

# Administration

### Creating the Systems That Display the Data, Follow the Figures, and File the Files

To get you up and running the right way, you have to put a system in place that everyone can rely on every day. Your administrative system covers all of the basics that your small business needs as a foundation to support all your daily activities, such as Operations, Finance, Sales, and Service. Without this foundation, you can't operate a successful business.

### Tracking Your Business Records

Someone in your office has to track all the business tasks, records, and related information. Let's take a look at the administrative items you need to keep track of:

1. Calendars and scheduling
2. Uniforms and lockers
3. Credit Cards – yours and theirs
4. Receptionist duties
5. Follow-up calls
6. Filing systems
7. Employee records
8. Billing records
9. Vendor contacts
10. Software – office and accounting
11. Meetings and agendas
12. Office equipment, books, industry publications
13. Lease agreement
14. Memberships, certifications and licenses
15. Insurance
16. Your business plan
17. IRS records

Even though certain of these items may sound obvious, nonetheless you need to have a system in place for tracking them.

**Calendars and Scheduling**

Calendars are mainly for appointments. You can use the standard, old-fashioned wall calendar or your computer or your smartphone, but don't just keep dates and appointments in your head. Your brain is the least reliable computer in the office.

My smartphone calendar works great when I'm out of the office or at home, but the calendar I refer to most in the office is the trusty little desktop At-A-Glance.

For scheduling, I use a whiteboard with dry erase markers, easily readable from across the room. You could also take advantage of a Microsoft Outlook or Google calendar, one that all of your employees can access from anywhere via cell phone. The good thing about computerized scheduling is that you can see what's happening tomorrow while you're doing other things.

In this constantly changing high-tech era, you should become familiar with some of the technology out there although many business owners still use methods other than a computer-based program to communicate.

One important note about scheduling in a service-oriented business, if you have employees in the field, you need to know where they are and how to reach them in case of a change in schedule or a cancelled appointment.

**Uniforms and Lockers**

If you provide uniforms for your employees, and I think you should, the size requirements change as fast as your turnover. For this reason, it may be advisable to hire a uniform company, like Cintas or UniFirst to quickly supply new, properly sized uniforms. You should provide lockers where your employees can regularly return their uniforms for laundering, or let them do their own cleaning at home – just make sure they look spiffy every day – no point in spending the bucks on this stuff if they look soiled and unkempt.

### Credit Cards – Yours and Theirs

For a service business, you and your key employees should have a company credit card to facilitate on-the-spot purchases or online orders. You may want to have several different card accounts, for example, one for office purchases, one for fuel, and one for equipment. It's important to track who's doing what with many cards floating around which is a good reason to check your bank account balances every day.

If you accept customer credit cards, and I think you should, you'll pay the merchant service organization somewhere between 1 percent and 3 percent on each sale. Take that into account when you price your products or services. Assign one employee, possibly your office manager, to process all the customer credit card charges. And remember, if cash flow is an issue, it will take from three to five business days for the cash to show up in your company bank account.

### Receptionist Duties

As part of your client-centered service, you must emphasize the human element in all of your business practices. This means a person must answer the phone during business hours. You can use an answering machine after hours and on weekends, but make sure someone in your office physically picks up the phone during the day – and not someone who sounds whiny, tired, or uninformed. That first impression may be the last impression.

### Follow-up Calls

Speaking of client-centered service, telephone calls are only second best to in-person communication. You and your employees should be primarily using the phone, not sending text messages or emails. Forget postcard follow-ups – they just get tossed. It's extremely important that you listen to your clients. Postcards don't listen to anything.

Call each of your clients back after they've purchased your product or service. Find out if they're happy with it and if there's anything else they need. Also, if you provide a product or service that needs periodic checkups or maintenance, use software to track your call-backs on a one-, two-, or three-year schedule.

### Filing Systems

Filing cabinets are essential. Label every file; keep the last two years worth of records in your office files and the rest in storage for up to seven years. Check the IRS regulations and shred the old files you aren't required to keep.

### Employee Records

You need to keep files on all your employees, including those no longer working for you. Typical information contained in these files is as follows:

1. Original employee application form
2. Hire date, wage, and salary increases with dates
3. Identification information, e.g., copies of driver's license and social security number
4. Infractions and bonuses
5. Certifications
6. Health information (as allowed by law), health insurance coverage
7. Vacation and benefits calculations
8. Company credit cards authorized for use
9. Employee handbook signature page, signed and dated by employee

### Billing Records

If you use accounting software, you should be tracking all of your clients to include the following information:

1. Contact information: name, address, phone (home/work/mobile), email

2. Estimates and invoices (both paid and unpaid), credits, gift certificates
3. A description of the product or service provided

### Vendor Contacts

Post a list of all of your vendor contact information. Include name, address, phones, email address, and payment terms (30-day, 60-day, etc.). This way, anyone in your office who is authorized to issue payment has access to this contact information. Set a limit, such as $300, that your employees can spend without your approval.

### Software – Office and Accounting

Different types of business software are available for PC and Mac users and some software will work on both operating systems. I have been using Windows for the last 15 years mainly because, at one time, the Windows-compatible software was less expensive and was used by most businesses. I don't recommend one operating system over the other, so choose whatever you prefer. While Macs can now run Windows software, my recommendations below are for the Windows operating system:

1. Microsoft Office – This includes Microsoft Word, Excel, and many other applications. We use Word for all our letters; all our spreadsheets are done using Excel. Also included in this Microsoft package is Outlook, which is the calendar and email program we use. Outlook can be accessed by your employees anytime, anywhere. And it includes a To Do list so you can get rid of all those sticky notes pasted on your screen. [WEB SEARCH: Microsoft Office 365]

   In addition to buying software on a CD, with the advent of the Cloud, more and more, businesses are creating many of their documents online. The Cloud is hosted on a remote server, not on your own computer.

2. Adobe Reader – This is an application that allows you to read PDF documents, which are documents that are originally created by the

sender using software that you may not have. As long as the sender has saved and sent you a PDF copy of their document, you can open it with Adobe Reader even if you don't have the sender's type of software on your computer. You can download Adobe Reader for free online.

3. Adobe Illustrator – This is a graphics program that allows you to draw darn near anything you can think of. With Illustrator, you can do designs for letterhead, business cards, and your website.

4. Adobe Photoshop Elements – This is the simplified version of Adobe Photoshop, the long-standing software used by professionals in the photo and journalism industries. This simplified version is easy to use and allows you to create great photos.

5. QuickBooks (by Intuit) – I have used this accounting software for years. Other programs are on the market and you may want to check them out, but QuickBooks has worked for us; our bookkeeper and accountant are able to easily work with QuickBooks files.

6. Anti-virus Software – Many choices are available. I have used McAfee AntiVirus, Norton Security, and Kaspersky Anti-Virus. Whatever you choose, install it immediately. Viruses can infect a computer at any time, and they are dangerous. We actually ended up tossing a computer because it was totally unfixable.

7. Customer Relationship Management (CRM) – If you want to track and manage all your customer interactions, you can invest in CRM software. Some of the bigger names in the industry who offer this type of software include Salesforce, ACT, and Microsoft Dynamics CRM. These are relatively expensive programs, often paid for on a monthly basis, so if you don't have a large clientele that you need to track, you might just keep all of your customer notes in your accounting software. In any event, you should be keeping regularly updated information on all of your customers.

Depending on the type of business you're in, the above-noted list may not meet your requirements. At the very least, if you're going to pick any of the above, I suggest that you go with Microsoft Office. I believe it's the most widely used of any type of software. Finally, look for industry-specific software that is designed for the type of business you own. [WEB SEARCH: Industry specific software for contractors, etc.]

## Meetings and Agendas

Avoid scheduling meetings for single issues. Hold all those individual items for a once-a-week agenda and invite only those who need to have the information. Ask the attendees to share the information with anyone whose attendance is not required.

Also consider holding a quarterly meeting with everyone in attendance. Share company updates, give out bonuses and awards, and invite a guest speaker whom the group will be interested in hearing. If you're not a good speaker, don't speak. Instead, invite someone who can facilitate the meeting in an informative, succinct, and engaging way. Never allow a meeting, any meeting, to go longer than an hour.

## Office Equipment, Books, and Industry Publications

Office equipment includes all of the obvious: computers, laptops, land lines, cell phones, computer servers, etc. Rather than buying these items one at a time, see if you can get a deal from one of the major manufacturers like Dell. For telephones, ATT, Comcast, T-Mobile and Sprint are constantly vying with each other for the best package deals. This would be one of the few times I'd recommend dealing with large companies; however, it may be difficult to change once you are contracted.

Invest in any important reference books that will keep you on the cutting edge of your type of business. The same thing goes for industry publications; in almost every case, they'll send them to you for free. The downside is that you'll probably start getting such publications from everyone under the sun.

## The Lease Agreement

Without a lease, the landlord can raise the rent to any amount and evict you with little or no notice. An oral agreement is only as good as the paper it's written on. Always get a written lease. You might consider showing it to an attorney to ensure you are fully protected.

## Memberships, Certifications, and Licenses

There's an industry group for almost every profession out there. Join the ones that sound legitimate, put their certificates on your wall, and print them on your brochures and business cards, even your website. Some of these groups can support you with a degree of professionalism and cutting-edge information. Membership often includes access to lower-priced items that you need to buy anyway.

For many occupations, actual certification may be required; in some states, you can't do a job for more than $500 without a contractor's license. Check your state and local regulations for license and certification requirements.

I recommend that you join the Better Business Bureau (BBB) in your area. Some potential customers really do their homework before contacting a business, and an A+ rating with the BBB will help.

## Insurance

You may be surprised to learn how many different kinds of insurance companies are available. You'll have to include most or all of the following in your budget: general liability insurance, Workers Compensation insurance, auto insurance, and health insurance. Since the rates for these can vary from year to year, you need to review all your insurance policies and insurance agents at least once a year. Regarding general liability insurance, you should have minimum coverage of $1 million. If you're using any subcontractors, you need to have proof of their insurance on file to ensure that they have adequate coverage.

## Your Business Plan

You might think you will need a business plan only at startup because if you're looking for a loan a lender can require it. That's not the only reason you need a business plan. In fact, you should do an updated plan every year. In addition to lender or investor requirements, you need a roadmap to plan the direction of your business. [WEB SEARCH: Sample business plans]

An example of a typical business plan follows.

## Executive Summary

The executive summary is a very brief description of your business that includes some of the items listed below. Write two or three paragraphs describing your business objective and how you're going to get there. Keep it short; this is just an overview.

## Company Summary

List here the names of each of your business owners and their percentage share of the business. Indicate whether you are a sole proprietor, partnership, or corporation.

## Market Analysis Summary

Are you a retail or a service business? Identify your local competition. Who will be your most likely customers (in other words, what customer types are you targeting)?

## Strategy and Implementation Summary

What is your competitive edge? How will you go about marketing your company? What is your forecast for sales revenue for the next 12 months?

## Management Summary

What employees are on board now and what employee types (by job description) will you be hiring in the next 12 months? Also provide an in-depth job description for yourself and for any partners.

## Financial Plan

What do you specifically plan to do with your loan or income (list a clear description by expense type)? What is your break-even point (how much do you need just to pay the bills)? If you have it, include your P&L statement and Balance Sheet.

The definition of a business plan is a description of how you plan to run your business. Some businesses just start pounding the nails, pruning the trees, or making the sandwiches, but there's a much more to it than that. Take the time to prepare a well-thought-out plan for success and review it on a regular basis; things may change without your knowledge and often much to your surprise. Be prepared.

## The IRS

You must pay your estimated quarterly taxes on time, and you should be setting aside funds for these estimated taxes, usually once every three months. This is a major cost of doing business, and you must take it into account on a regular basis. Plug it into your budget. And make sure you use the right forms; there are only a few thousand of them.

While you may complete your own personal income tax returns at home, you should have an accountant prepare your business returns. They are more complex and you may never have seen many of the additional forms or know how to complete them correctly.

## Leadership

As the owner of a small business, your role is to lead your business to prosperity and the fulfillment of your vision. Your contribution to the success or failure of your business lies in your willingness to look into the future. Here's a story that Bill Ross, my business consultant, related to me:

He had gone to lunch, and while waiting to order his food, he observed an employee filling the salt shakers at every table. There were two cash registers in the restaurant but only one of them was manned. A long line was starting to form behind the one open register and he asked the employee if opening the second register was possible. The employee was actually the owner of the restaurant.

You are the owner and leader of your company. You can't be filling salt shakers. One of your employees can handle that role, take out the trash, clean the restrooms, and bus tables. You must prepare strategies and make plans to fulfill them, and create ideas that will keep your company on a stable footing, growing and providing increased opportunities for both your employees and your customers. You can't just be the guy behind the cash register. Maybe that was your job when you worked for someone else, but it's not your job now.

Learn from the past, but more importantly, focus on the future. Create the vision that leads to your company's success. Ideas may be a dime a dozen, but without them, don't expect results. Honor everyone's ideas then push for proof of positive results. The hit rate for achieving a great result may be only 1 in 10, but without your vision and persistence, it may turn out to be zero.

Now that you are prepared to assemble a solid business plan to complete Step One, this is a good time to introduce you to our first case study. I interviewed 20 owners of small businesses to gather insight into the value of the five step process outlined in this book. You will find most of these case studies in the appendix at the end of the book, but I have selected several of them for inclusion in each of the chapters.

Let's meet our first interviewee. He started a small IT (information technology) company seven years ago, a business which is now enjoying a satisfactory profit.

The Little Business Book Step One - Administration

Category: IT Managed Service Provider

## Cloud 1 Solutions

*By providing managed services to companies of varying sizes, Cloud 1 helps those businesses focus on revenue and their core competencies. Mike Wiechmann, who founded Cloud 1 Solutions, comes from an in-depth IT background working with major corporations on both coasts. Mike says his business model delivers real value by allowing staff to focus on revenue-related activities instead of overhead (or non-value activities, like trying to figure out how to get your email to work).*

Year started (or took over) the business: *2008*
Amount of startup capital (either a loan or your own money): *$10,000*
Obtained startup capital from: *Mike's own money*
Number of employees at startup: *1*    Number of employees today: *3*
Gross revenue first fiscal year: *$20,000*   Gross revenue last fiscal year: *$500,000*
How many years did it take before you started making a <u>satisfactory</u> profit: *5*

Most valuable idea or action you've taken: *I found a great business consultant who helped me stay on track with my targeted business model which is long-term managed services rather than one-at-a-time fixit projects.*

Least valuable idea or action you've taken: *Selling out to pay the bills when we first started – doing things like running cable and installing phone lines. We don't do that anymore – that's not our expertise.*

What's more important?

- The value of your services: <u>*X*</u>    Or    - The price of your services: _____

- Why? *If you can't show value, you have to sell price and we don't sell based on price.*

- Return customers: *X*    Or    - Advertising: _____

- Why? *Not only return customers, but our whole model is based on long-term customer retention.*

- Cash flow: *X*    Or    - Credit rating: _____

- Why? *Not having credit has never stopped us. The minute you "need" a loan, you won't get it.*

- Understanding your financials *X*    Or    - Being good at what you do: _____

- Why? *You can be good at what you do and go bankrupt.*

Best advice for a new owner (or one who's not yet successful):

*Don't start a company just to have a job. When I was employed by someone else, I often worked from 6AM to 9PM. No more. Now I have my own real company and I set the time frames.*

*A new owner needs to determine what "kind" of company they want to run. There are three kinds: Marketing companies, Sales companies, and Operations companies. Get a clear picture of what your company purpose is. Are you in business primarily to market your product, to sell your product, or to build your product?*

*Finally, keep these next two items in the forefront of your company every day: (a) Listening is critically important, and (b) a little humility will take you a long way.*

Here are the highlights of Step One for your quick review.

## ADMINISTRATION HIGHLIGHTS

- Maintain a filing system for all your business records.

- Use a dry-erase board for calendars, notices, and scheduling.

- Keep accurate billing records by using accounting software.

- Keep in-depth records of all your employee's activities.

- Avoid meetings to discuss single issues or that exceed 1 hour.

- Employ commonly used software such as Microsoft Office and QuickBooks.

- Maintain an adequate amount of general liability insurance.

- Review and update your business plan annually.

- Pay your estimated quarterly taxes on time.

- Make follow-up calls to all your customers at periodic intervals.

## STEP TWO

# Operations

### Hiring and Training Employees for
### Work in a Safe and Sound Environment.

Step Two involves the relationship between you and your employees; how you hire and fire them, provide Workers Compensation insurance for them, and observe all the labor law requirements of your state. Let's begin with an important note about hiring.

### Hire Slowly, Fire Quickly

Many small business owners hire their employees too quickly and then take forever to let a bad employee go, even after it's obvious he or she isn't up to the task. In Jim Collin's classic, "Good to Great," he says that good-to-great leaders start by "getting the right people on the bus and the wrong people off the bus."

You should start your hiring process by first making a list of the qualifications that your employees must have, and then turn that list into a specific job description. Use that job description as your ad copy in the local newspaper and on the web. A number of websites will post your job availability (for a fee).

Check out Indeed.com and Monster.com, and there's probably some local employment websites that are targeted to your geographic area. [WEB SEARCH: Employee job search]

One of the first things you need to do is put together an Employee Handbook. If you've always done everything yourself, you're probably clueless about current laws and regulations for hiring and firing. At the very least, go to the web and find out what your state's Department of Labor requirements are for employers.

## Employee Handbook

Developing your own employee handbook and having your employees sign it will save you when an employee comes to you with an odd request; many do, and often they know more about their rights than you do. Here are some of the items your handbook should address:

1. Definition of full-time employees and part-time employees
2. Job duties with in-depth descriptions
3. Probationary period, sick pay, paid time off, holidays
4. Benefits, Insurance, Workers Compensation
5. Performance evaluations
6. Definition of company property
7. Employee conduct, dress code, drug and alcohol use
8. Wages, regular time, overtime, bonuses, pay scale
9. Health and safety
10. Termination

What follows is a discussion of employee handbook items; note that these elements may not be legally appropriate for your business. You need to do your own in-depth research, based on government requirements for what is legal in your state and what is not.

### Full-time employees and part-time employees

Full-time employees are those scheduled to work a 40-hour workweek. Full-time employees are eligible for the employee benefits described in the employee handbook. Part-time employees work less than 40 hours per week and are not eligible for employee benefits.

### A typical job duty description

Sales Manager – Must have a minimum number of years sales experience working with customers in your industry. In addition to working with existing accounts, the sales manager will develop sales presentations and focus on bringing in new business. Other duties include submitting sales reports and assisting with customer complaints. A valid driver's license is required.

## Probationary period, sick pay, paid time off, holidays

Note: Check your state requirements regarding these items. Don't just guess. Verify.

The probationary period gives you an opportunity to assess a new employee before entering into an employment agreement. The probationary period is usually the first 90 days of employment. No employee benefits are available during this trial period. Completion of this period may not guarantee continued employment. In some states, an "at-will employment" contract clause will allow either the employer or employee to terminate employment for any reason as long as the stated period of advance notice is given.

You can define many types of pay that you will make available to your employees. Additional pay examples include paid family leave, jury duty, military leave, and time off for voting. All types of leave must be requested by the employee in writing. With sick pay, you should determine how many days you are willing to pay an employee who is absent.

Sick pay: Depending on state law, employees are allowed paid sick leave as part of the paid time off provisions in the employee handbook. Since paid time off can include any number of paid allowable absences, e.g., vacation pay, jury duty, sick pay, etc., you must specifically state what types of paid absences are covered.

Paid time off (PTO): After the probationary period, full-time employees may be entitled to 5 days of paid time off annually and may accrue one additional day at the end of each 12-month period of fulltime employment to a maximum of ten years of employment. In the absence of state laws specifying the exact number of paid time off days that are required, you may set your own schedule for paid time off days.

Holidays: Many companies observe the following paid holidays: January 1 (New Year's Day), Memorial Day, July 4 (Independence Day), Labor Day, Thanksgiving Day, and Christmas Day.

## Benefits, insurance, Workers Compensation

The scope of employee benefits is extensive, and this book is not intended to provide the kind of in-depth study of the countless available benefits that you'd like, or may be required, to offer to your employees. You need a professional to make recommendations. It could be your insurance agent. Some of the more well-known benefits include: health insurance, retirement plans, 401(k), and profit sharing.

Offering various benefits to your employees could add more to their base pay. In the accounting business, this is often referred to as "burden" and it can amount to a notable increase in your costs.

At the present time, the question of health insurance has become problematic. Depending on the number of full-time workers you employ, you may be required by law to provide it. Talk to your insurance agent to determine your legal requirements. If you can afford to pay all or part of your employee's health insurance premiums, they will greatly appreciate it. New job applicants almost always ask if you offer insurance coverage.

Now here's the big one – Workers Compensation. At present, almost all states require some form of Workers Compensation insurance. It's not a matter of choice, you must provide it.

Don't play fast and loose with this one. If one of your employees is injured on the job and you don't have Workers Compensation insurance, it could wipe out your company financially. [WEB SEARCH: (your state) Workers Compensation Requirements]

Finally, I can't overemphasize the need for you to be thoroughly familiar with all of the various ramifications of Human Resource Law and Labor Law in your state. My recommendation is that you hire a professional to help you put together an accurate and enforceable employee handbook. Do not copy the examples listed here into your handbook; use them only as a reference prior to formulating your own.

## Performance evaluations

Employees want to know how they're doing, and a periodic performance review is the most organized way to stay on top of giving raises or tracking poor service. It also provides you with a paper trail that documents an employee's activity in the event you need to terminate them.

## Company property

You may provide your employees with uniforms and equipment necessary for them to perform their job in line with your company's image and reputation. This might include the use of a company vehicle. Use this provision to specify guidelines for the care and maintenance of company property and what items need to be returned upon termination.

## Employee conduct, dress code, drug and alcohol use

Drug and alcohol use can be pervasive and can lead to accidents on the job. Specify what is unacceptable. You may choose to purchase uniforms or reimburse your employees for wearing the apparel you require. Since employee conduct speaks volumes about the nature of your business, you should specify any conduct you consider to be unacceptable. Failure to adhere to stated company policy should be included in their written performance evaluations.

## Wages, regular time, overtime, bonuses, pay scale

Calculation of regular pay versus overtime pay can become a bone of contention and you need a clear reading of how your state's regulations define each one. Use their definition in your handbook. Overtime pay may be required for both daily and weekly total hours worked.

If you're going to institute some type of bonus program, make sure you examine both the best case and worst case scenarios. Particularly if you're using a percentage figure to calculate the bonus, it's possible you may actually end up losing money by paying bonuses. Whatever your stated formula is, you must honor it.

You should consider distributing to all of your employees a printed pay scale that ties individual job descriptions to various rates of pay (hourly, weekly, or monthly). This will tell them what they need to do to get a raise and/or move into a new position.

**Health and safety**

Workers Compensation premiums are usually based on the amount of your payroll and include a risk assessment of your company's safety performance. If you have a less-than stellar safety record or you're in a high-risk industry, you will pay considerably more for Workers Compensation insurance. That's why it pays to keep your people safe.

Put a regular safety training program in place, something like a weekly tailgate meeting or an in-office video presentation. It could even be conducted online. If you've never heard the term Occupational Health and Safety Administration (OSHA), you need to check it out before they arrive on your doorstep in answer to a safety violation.

**Termination**

There are several different types of employee termination: Involuntary (you fire them), Reduction in Force (you lay them off), or Voluntary (they quit). Whichever one comes into play, you will need to prepare certain documents within a certain timeframe that include delivery of a final paycheck. Your employee's signature and consent may also be required. Improper handling of an employee's termination could result in a lawsuit or lengthy investigation by a government agency. Stay on top of this one.

**Operations Manager**

If you're a sole proprietor, you may have to double as your own operations manager, but if you have more than one or two employees, you need someone besides yourself who can act in a management capacity either as an operations manager or a general manager. You'll send your stress level through the roof if you try to handle everything all by yourself.

One of the characteristics of small business owners is their naïve belief that they can singularly manage the whole ball of wax. If you want to speed going out of business, keep thinking that way. Otherwise, bring in someone who can handle the operations aspect of your business. And don't say you can't afford it. Unless, of course, you believe you can handle all of the following items on your own:

1. Hiring
2. Firing
3. Sales training
4. Safety training
5. Equipment purchases
6. Equipment training
7. Maintenance and repair
8. Licenses and permits
9. Scheduling
10. Communications
11. Employee accident reports
12. Emergency medical aid
13. Employee relations and discipline
14. Inventory and parts supply
15. Store and yard security
16. Production control

As an owner, if you can do all of the above yourself, then you should be featured on the cover of Business Week.

## Notable Aspects of Operations Management

### Hiring employees

As noted earlier, you should be very careful in hiring new employees. Develop an Employment Application form which requests references that you can contact. Know that previous employers may be limited by law regarding what types of information they can disclose to you about an applicant. The same restrictions may apply to you once an employee leaves your company.

Arrange an appointment for an in-person interview with the new applicant and a possible second follow-up interview by someone else on your staff like your Operations Manager. You can also do drug testing and a background check subject to your state's requirements. I strongly recommend both.

### Firing employees

This is fraught with all kinds of potential problems. Understand your state's regulations regarding termination before you do anything. Additionally, if one of your employees is injured on the job and can't work because of doctor's orders, you may have to take them back, even months later, if the doctor releases them to modified duty; and you could be required to pay them their original wage just to sit around the office and watch training videos all day.

### Safety training

Even though you may have Workers Compensation insurance which covers your employees if they're injured on the job, you still need to take all reasonable steps to provide employees with in-depth and up-to-date safety training. Aside from the legal and regulatory consequences of an unsafe work environment, the last thing you need in the middle of your day is a phone call informing you that one of your employees has just been injured on the job.

IMPORTANT FOOTNOTE: If you're a sole proprietor or a partnership, you may want to consider converting your company to a corporation, maybe an S-Corp or a Limited Liability Company (LLC) [WEB SEARCH: Types of corporations] as a way to protect yourself from personal liability in the event of a lawsuit. However, it should be noted that corporate status doesn't automatically shield you from personal liability. In certain situations, courts can ignore limited liability by "piercing the corporate veil" and holding the officers, directors, and shareholders personally liable for the company's obligations.

## Maintenance and repair

Don't neglect the condition of your office or yard equipment, particularly vehicles, or your eventual repair and replacement costs could escalate well beyond what you have budgeted. Set up a system to track maintenance and repairs and review it regularly. A company whose equipment is down can't produce revenue.

## Licenses and permits

You may be required to have a current (annual) business license for every city you work in. Municipalities rely, to some extent, on the revenue from these licenses, and they'll be in touch with you if your licenses aren't current. If permits are required for anything you do, don't do any work without them or the governing agency may "red tag" you and require that you start all over from scratch.

## Employee relations and discipline

You should keep personnel records that include performance reviews, vacation requests, absentee records, accident reports, and anything else that's pertinent to your employees. This provides the "paper trail" necessary to keep you from getting in trouble because of employment issues. Ignorance of the law is no excuse. A well-maintained employee file will keep you protected.

Establish a clear and fair methodology for handling infractions as well as rewards. If an employee damages client or company property, you may not be able to deduct the cost from their paycheck since some states consider this to be "the cost of doing business." You may have to absorb the loss yourself.

### What's Good About Employees?

By now you're probably thinking "forget the employees, I'll do it myself." A really great employee makes you proud of what you've accomplished, and much of your success is because of them. You can't do it all and you're foolish to think you can.

I believe there's more to building a great crew than just encouraging teamwork. Even among the best of teams there are standouts – the ones you want to encourage and listen to and learn from. A great employee isn't just a team player; he or she is a game-changer. While team players support the group, game-changers are in it primarily for themselves. They may, on occasion, go beyond the duties of their job description and you may need to rein them in, but they think like owners; they're creative, motivated, and passionate.

If there's anything I've learned about employees it's that you can't motivate them; they can only motivate themselves. Sure, you can dazzle them with rewards and bonuses, but truly great employees are self-starters – just like you. And one day they may be running their own business – just like you. While you have such workers, consider yourself fortunate because they're the fuel that runs your engine.

A company team is different from a success team. Success teams usually consist of you and only a handful of others. Some of your employees may be there primarily for a paycheck. Nurture the great ones; they'll get you through the bad times and share with you the good times. You're the visionary – they're the vision.

Share your dreams and doubts with your employees. The good ones will join you on your road to success.

Our next interviewee is a doctor who has become the green optometrist in town. Wait until you see what he has done with his office.

**Category: Optometrist**

## GIANNOTTI VISION CARE

*This is a study of a professional who truly advocates working on your business as well as in your business. Dr. Anthony Giannotti has* moved and upgraded his facility three times over the years, and not only has his practice increased, his office systems, technology, and interior design has become a notable focus of his many loyal customers.

     Dr. Giannotti provides the kind of personalized care that I speak of in this book; client-centered service is right at the top of his list. He relishes creating a unique experience, and when he converted to what he calls a medical model encompassing both eye care and eye wear, and matched that with an office lit by solar tubes and other natural lighting, cork floors, recycled materials, and the most eye-relaxing wall colors, he also became the green optometrist in town.

Year started (or took over) the business: *1981*
Amount of startup capital (either a loan or your own money): *$70,000*
Obtained startup capital from: *Bank of America*
Number of employees at startup: *1*   Number of employees today: *8*
Gross revenue first fiscal year: *$49,000*   Gross revenue last fiscal year: *n/a*
How many years did it take before you started making a satisfactory profit: *Not yet*

Most valuable idea or action you've taken: *Moving the office. I did a strategic review of my business, including looking far into the future and considering an exit strategy. Then I hired an experienced office manager because I knew I couldn't do it all myself.*

Least valuable idea or action you've taken: *I should have moved and expanded my office sooner. And I also should have joined the service clubs I'm now a member of much sooner.*

What's more important?

- The value of your services: *X*     Or    - The price of your services: _____

- Why? *I don't try to compete with Costco or Walmart and I'd much rather cultivate great relationships.*

- Return customers: *X*      Or     - Advertising: _____

- Why? *If you take good care of your return customers, you'll develop those long-term relationships so important to sustaining your business.*

- Cash flow:  *X*              Or   - Credit rating: _____

- Why? *If you have good cash flow, you'll have a good credit rating. Plus, I have a great relationship with my bank.*

- Understanding your financials  *X*     Or   - Being good at what you do: _____

- Why? *You can be brilliant, but if you don't know your financials, you can lose money. Besides that, you need to continually project your growth in order to get a good assessment of where your business is going.*

Best advice for a new owner (or one who's not yet successful):

*Surround yourself with smart people. I once attempted to do a relocation of my practice on my own. It was simply too much dealing with all the requirements and red tape. I hired a project manager who interviewed sixteen contractors and eight different banks and he pulled the whole thing together for me.*

*Moral of the story: don't try to do everything yourself.*

*Think about taking some strategic planning courses. I belong to a wisdom sharing group that looks at all my numbers and sets benchmarks.*

*Finally, enjoy your overall service ethic. I did a medical mission to Guatemala and had the best time ever.*

Here are the highlights of Step Two for your quick review.

## OPERATIONS HIGHLIGHTS

- Hire slowly, fire quickly.

- Develop an in-depth employee handbook.

- Don't pay your employees cash under the table.

- Obtain Workers Compensation insurance.

- Be aware of the naïve belief that an owner can handle everything.

- If you have several employees, consider hiring an Operations Manager.

- Know the ramifications of labor law in your state or consult an HR firm.

- Provide ongoing equipment and safety training.

- Nurture key employees to become part of your Success Team.

- Share your vision with all of your employees.

## Step Three

# Finance

**How to Read the Numbers and Make a Profit**

Finance is probably the most-ignored field in the small business owner's playbook. Why? Unless your business is accounting, your specialty is probably something other than numbers. You might be a great builder, baker, or candlestick maker, but the science of money, beyond what you need to keep food on the table, is just not your thing. *Caveat – it needs to become your thing right now.*

When you decided to open your own business, you probably did so because you're really good at something; but just because you're really good at something does not a business make. If you're an auto mechanic, you might love tinkering with transmissions, but you can tinker yourself right out of business if you don't get on top of the numbers immediately. Build accounting into your startup plan. You'll be pleasantly surprised that it's not that hard to learn. It doesn't matter if you flunked math in high school. Understanding financials doesn't require excellence in math.

In the following pages, we're going to look at how to price your goods or services, what types of accounting software are available, learn to read a Profit and Loss Statement, hire a bookkeeper, how to make a profit, target your revenue goals, how to budget and handle payroll and loans.

If you don't make finances your thing, you're going to drop right into a hole. You shouldn't be scared to take a peek at your financials – and I'll show you how to do that, quick and easy.

**Pricing Goods and Services**

When I first opened my business, I looked around to see how much my competitors were charging, then set my prices just a little lower.

Wrong. This completely contradicts the value-over-price objective. It's not about price. You're not going to win hearts and minds just by being cheaper than everyone else. Instead, you'll attract mainly bargain hunters. Such customers are not the bread and butter of small business.

Before you can set your prices, you need to decide how much profit you'd like to make. Do you want to make 5 percent more than you spend, or 10 percent? This is usually referred to as *net profit* or "the bottom line." Basically, you need to make more money than you spend.

First, put together an estimate of all your expenses. Then, price your goods or services to bring in something more than your total expenses. In my book, a profitable business makes money; it doesn't lose it – ever.

Just to give you a little jump start on the value of understanding your profit & loss statement (P&L), the bookkeeper you hire will put all your expenses into your P&L, and you'll be surprised at how much money you spend. At this first stage of estimating your expenses, there are some costs you don't even know about. Figure expenses high and count on spending more than your first guess.

Check your competitor's prices to get a sense of what the general market is accustomed to. Many of your competitors still may be using the old pricing method of offering the lowest bid in order to close the deal. While you need to know your competitors' prices, you shouldn't try to match them. This just sets up a situation that has each of you continually dropping your price to beat the other. Ba-a-a-ad example to follow. It's not just a matter of closing the deal; you also have to make a profit.

The big difference between big business and small business is that the objective of big business is to keep *lowering* their prices to beat the competition. Often it's not *their* money, it's their stockholders money or they have access to a major line of credit. Small businesses shouldn't borrow money to play the low price game. It will only put you further in debt.

## Typical Expenses

- ☐ Advertising
- ☐ Telephone
- ☐ Rent
- ☐ Legal/accounting
- ☐ Repairs/maintenance
- ☐ Software
- ☐ Memberships

- ☐ Fuel
- ☐ Dues/subscriptions
- ☐ Taxes
- ☐ Owner's salary
- ☐ Loan payments
- ☐ Outside services
- ☐ Postage

- ☐ Utilities
- ☐ Donations
- ☐ Insurance
- ☐ Office supplies
- ☐ Interest
- ☐ Bank charges
- ☐ Travel/entertainment

You'll notice I haven't included the cost of your inventory. That, along with employee payroll, actually shows up in a different section of your P&L listed as Cost of Goods Sold (COGS). The reason is that the top line of your P&L shows your total sales followed by the *direct* cost of selling your product or service. For example, without your inventory and employees, you would have no sales. Inventory and employee payroll is a direct cost related to your product or service, unlike rent, taxes or bank charges, etc. When you deduct your direct cost of goods sold from your total sales, what is left is your Gross Profit. When you further deduct all of the typical expenses listed above, what is left is your Net Profit, the "bottom line."

Once you have the total outflow, you can add 5 or 10 percent (or any percentage) onto that total to set your selling price.

One caveat here – Don't limit yourself to making 5 or 10 percent more than your total expenses. That's really just for starters. In the future, as you do your annual growth planning, you may want to make more profit. If you can make 20 percent or 30 percent more, go for it. Then save those bucks as insurance for the next recession. More than a few of the case studies presented in the appendix wish they would have done that.

The Little Business Book Step Three - Finance

## Accounting Systems

The accounting practice that small business owners adopt needs to keep your involvement with the financials quick and easy. To achieve this, hire a bookkeeper and purchase an accounting software program.

Back in the dark ages, small businesses used a ledger, noting by hand all their income and expenses into a general journal. I strongly recommend starting with a good software program right from day one. Nowdays, one well-known software program for small business is QuickBooks.

However, accountants have told me they don't like it because it doesn't follow the traditional accounting format, and they often have to move expense categories or add additional items for tax purposes. [WEB SEARCH: Small Business Accounting Software]

At the very least, you'll need to generate a P&L statement which will become your monthly money bible. And you'll need to regularly record all of your income and expenses to see at a glance how the business is doing. If you need a loan, all lenders will require a copy of your most recent P&L and balance sheet.

## The Profit and Loss Statement and Balance Sheet

The P&L statement, sometimes referred to as the Income Statement or Statement of Operations, is your regular reference point for finances. It will tell you very quickly what you need more of and what's out of whack. But to be financially successful, you yourself need some quick ways to check the health of your business.

The P&L statement is comprised of five key parts: sales, cost of goods sold, gross profit, expenses, and net income. Let's look at each of the five parts.

**1 – Sales** (sometimes referred to as Income or Gross Revenue). This is every dime that comes into your business. For quick reference, it can be broken down into subcategories such as sales, services, royalties, etc.

**2 – Cost of Goods Sold** (COGS). This is your direct cost to produce or acquire everything you sell. It includes the cost of labor and material used to produce your product or service.

**3 – Gross Profit.** When you subtract the COGS from your Sales, you get your Gross Profit. This is what's left after you pay the direct cost of your goods and services. You can derive an important number from your Gross Profit – your Profit Margin – usually expressed as a percentage. Example:

| | |
|---|---|
| Income from all sales or service | $50,000 |
| Cost of goods (or services) sold | -$30,000 |
| Gross profit | $20,000 |
| Profit margin | 40% |

Note: To calculate the profit margin percentage, divide gross profit by income.

**4 – Expenses** (also known as below the line or operating expenses or overhead). Here's where your office staff payroll shows up, along with rent, utilities, advertising, etc.

**5 – Net Income.** This is your profit, what's left after you've paid everything.

### Sample Profit and Loss Statement (for a full year)

| | |
|---|---|
| Sales | $300,000 |
| Cost of Goods Sold | $150,000 |
| Gross Profit | $150,000 |
| | |
| Expenses | |
|     Salaries (office staff and owner's salary) | $100,000 |

| | |
|---|---:|
| Utilities | $3,000 |
| Insurance | $7,000 |
| Taxes (local) | $3,000 |
| Advertising | $2,000 |
| Interest on a loan | $3,000 |
| Miscellaneous | $2,000 |
| | |
| Total expenses | $120,000 |
| | |
| Net income | $30,000 |

The profit margin on this sample P&L statement is 50 percent ($150,000 gross profit divided by $300,000 sales). For brevity, I left some items off the above example. In fact, your P&L statement may have many more entries than shown above.

Also, there's another even more important percentage than can be calculated here. If someone asks what your net income is, you can say 10 percent. $30,000 is your net income, or profit. You made a 10 percent profit in one year. But that's not all you made; remember, you also paid yourself a salary in the Expenses section.

For certain types of corporations, the government may tax both your salary (as personal income) and your net income (as business income). It can get expensive.

There's one other footnote about the two accounting methods the IRS will accept. You must choose one of these two methods: Cash Basis or Accrual Basis. Your bookkeeper may not know, so ask your accountant which one is best for your business. Here are the differences:

CASH BASIS – On your P&L statement, you will record your income in the month that you receive it and your expenses in the month that you pay your bills.

ACCRUAL BASIS – On your P&L statement, you will record your income in the month that your customer signs the agreement (even though you may not provide the product or service in that month or collect the payment in that month). The same thing applies to payment of your expenses; you record the payment in the month that you incur the bill, even though you might not actually pay the bill until sometime in the future.

Your accountant can explain how it all works. If you're using QuickBooks, it takes just one click to switch from cash to accrual on your computer screen, and when you make the switch you'll notice that all the numbers change slightly.

The other important financial statement is the Balance Sheet. You probably won't refer to it as often as your P&L statement, but your accountant and bookkeeper will. Entries that show up on the Balance Sheet are Current Assets and Liabilities, Cash on Hand, Notes Payable, Long-term Loans, and Credit Card Debt. There can be more items than listed here; your accountant and bookkeeper will know and add all of the necessary Balance Sheet items. [WEB SEARCH: Sample Balance Sheet]

Accountants earn more than bookkeepers, but you will be working with both. An accountant will prepare your income tax returns and advise you regarding your business's financial health. An accountant will also advise your bookkeeper on how to make the proper entries on your P&L statement and Balance Sheet. Your bookkeeper will enter all your financial data on the appropriate statements.

If you're trying to determine your ongoing cash flow, you need numbers from both the P&L statement and Balance Sheet. If you're making monthly loan payments, they will not show up on the P&L statement; only the interest will. So if you're tracking your daily or weekly cash flow to find out if you can pay your bills or not (I track mine daily) you need access to both the P&L statement and the Balance Sheet.

There is an additional way to track your cash flow using an Excel spreadsheet. I use these spreadsheets *in addition to* my accounting software. For tracking cash flow, which I track daily, I use a spreadsheet that I call my Morning Report. It shows this morning's bank balance, all the bills I'm going to pay that day, and all the money I'm going to collect that day.

If you don't want to learn Excel, you should at least have someone in your company who can monitor your cash flow. The biggest number you'll have to deal with each week is payroll, and you don't want to bounce your employees' paychecks.

## Why You Need To Hire a Bookkeeper

One of the best and least expensive investments you can make in your business is hiring a bookkeeper. Once a week they'll grab your bills and drop everything into your P&L statement (in the right place) for you. So, even though you need to understand the numbers, you don't have to input them yourself – your bookkeeper can do all that for you. I don't recommend trying to do everything we've just covered by yourself; get a bookkeeper and an accountant, if only on a limited basis. There are just too many things that can go wrong if you do it yourself.

## How to Use the Numbers

I had the opportunity to interview a bookkeeper, Kathy Greenwood, about her experience with not only accounting software but finance in general. As part of her 27-year career with bookkeeping for construction companies and several other industries, she graduated from handwritten general bookkeeping journals to software that proved to be more advantageous to company owners.

She has helped a number of startups and nonprofits and has spent time troubleshooting financial problems in businesses where management was unfamiliar with the critical aspects of understanding the books. During our interview, she was able to report the highlights of the bookkeeping process and its benefits to owners. Here's a brief excerpt from that interview:

Author: What is the main difference between the handwritten bookkeeping method and computer software?

Bookkeeper: *The yellow notepad method is rather prehistoric. My handwritten entries were done using Safeguard manual forms for checking account and payroll, accounts receivable, and accounts payable. It's possible for a small company to use this method, along with a calculator, to track their financials, but this type of bookkeeping doesn't yield financial reports, which small business owners must learn to read and use to keep their business on track. At the very least, you need to have a quick way of finding out whether you're being embezzled. You should have two people in your business familiar with and capable of running the accounting software.*

*Eventually, I began putting all of my entries on various Excel spreadsheets, and I still use spreadsheets for capturing all kinds of data.*

Author: What was the difference when you started using software?

Bookkeeper: *To begin with, one keystroke goes everywhere you want it to go. With one push of a button you can send that data to payroll, accounts payable, accounts receivable, job costing, maintenance, or anywhere else you might want to generate a report. When you enter an expense, let's say for an inventory item, that same entry will also alert you in the future when it's time to reorder. It also tells you what job that item is attached to, as well as including that item in the job costing report. Because of this integration, you don't need to rely on just spreadsheets; instead, you simply plug in a code number for a particular item or task. In the situation just mentioned, the employee handling the item or task would write that code number on their timecard.*

Author: What is your key reason for using accounting software?

Bookkeeper: *Reports. This is absolutely invaluable. An owner can use a report to update inventory, see the number of hours spent on a job, review all the aspects of job costing in depth, and learn how to do more accurate bidding based on the information gleaned from past reports.*

A recent article on cash flow which appeared on the website, Chron.com, written by Diana Wicks for Demand Media, ("The Most Important Financial Report for a Small Business") mentions "When starting out a small business, entrepreneurs may find it quite confusing to determine which reports are important and how to read these financial reports. The cash flow statement is arguably the most important of a small business' financial reports. The cash flow breaks down the information in the balance sheet and income statement into simpler data. A small business owner should report his cash flow on a monthly basis. This is especially true because small businesses experience hardship in raising and generating cash as they start up."

Here's a sample cash flow statement done in Microsoft Excel, one of five programs included in the Microsoft Office Home and Business software.

### SAMPLE CASH FLOW STATEMENT

| Month | January | February | March | Totals |
|---|---|---|---|---|
| Revenue | $30,000.00 | $20,000.00 | $40,000.00 | $90,000.00 |
| **Expenses** | | | | |
| Cost of Goods Sold | $15,000.00 | $16,000.00 | $18,000.00 | $49,000.00 |
| Overhead | $6,000.00 | $6,000.00 | $9,000.00 | $21,000.00 |
| Total Expenses | $21,000.00 | $22,000.00 | $27,000.00 | $70,000.00 |
| Cash Flow | $9,000.00 | -$2,000.00 | $13,000.00 | $20,000.00 |
| Beginning Check Acct. Bal. | $2,000.00 | $11,000.00 | $9,000.00 | |
| Ending Check Acct. Bal. | $11,000.00 | $9,000.00 | $22,000.00 | |

### Forms of Payment

*Cash or check* – in 15 years, I have received maybe three bad checks.

*Credit card* – you'll pay 2-3 percent in merchant service fees on every sale, so it could be costly if it's a big sale ($10,000 sale = $300 fee).

*Online payment* – usually by credit card, but it could be a bank draft.

*Trade or barter* – don't be averse to doing this occasionally, especially if you're in a cash flow crunch.

Particularly if your cash flow is really tight, keep in mind that you *will* have customers every month who "forget" to send you the payment on time as agreed. It may take two or three phone calls to collect the money, and you may incur overdraft charges on your own bank account to cover checks you've already written. Another caveat: Banks generally increase their fees for overdrafts every year.

Before the 2008 recession, many commercial accounts were accustomed to not paying their bills for 30 to 60 days. That's no longer the case, in spite of what your customer may argue. You are not a bank; you cannot carry them just because they have a cash flow problem of their own. State your payment terms clearly at the beginning of your transaction. Mine has always been "payment upon completion."

Be very clear about this with your customers right from the get-go. State it up front and put it in **bold** print on your contract. If you fail to handle this at the outset, you may find yourself in a frustrating and costly cash flow predicament.

### Target Revenue Goals

Every month, or at least annually, you need to set goals for how much income you expect to receive. These goals, usually set monthly can be based in part, on your projection of recurring monthly expenses. Probably more important in terms of your vision of the future, you need to set income goals that will push you to increase your annual revenue for the following three years. Also, when that day comes that it's time to sell your business, the selling price will be based primarily on your profits. The buyer will want to see your P&L statements for the last two or three years, and they'll be looking at (1) your bottom-line profit each year, and (2) how much you've taken home every year for yourself as a salary or distribution.

You should spend time every month reassessing your revenue goals. It's not just about increasing your income, because if your income goes up, more than likely your expenses will go up, too. You may have to hire more employees or purchase more vehicles and equipment, for example. That leads right into the next section on budgeting.

## Budgeting

At least annually you should prepare a 12-month budget that sets forth every type of income you estimate you'll receive and every expense you might incur each month. While this monthly budget is only an estimate, you could base it on your historical income and expenses from the last several years. If you're a new startup, figure your income on the low side and your expenses on the high side.

You could use your P&L statement as the format for your budget, but you must also include items that show up only on your balance sheet, such as long-term loan payments. I'll refer again to the use of Excel spreadsheets for doing your budget.

## Payroll

You can handle payroll yourself, but as the bookkeeper, Kathy Greenwood, notes, you can easily build payroll into your accounting system and tie it to job costing. There are all kinds of payroll expenses you'll have to include for each employee. Let me rattle off a partial list: employer portion of Social Security and Medicare taxes, employer paid holidays, employer paid state and federal unemployment taxes, Worker Compensation insurance, employer portion of health and other types of insurance, employer contributions toward savings and profit-sharing plans, and employer-paid sick days and bonus pay. Even though you may enjoy doing this on your own, why not let your software do it all for you?

You'll also have to fill out forms that the government provides, for example, the W-4 where you calculate your employees' tax withholding and the number of deductions they're claiming.

With the right software, you could have your bookkeeper or your accountant do all this, but let me offer one more alternative. I've been using a payroll service for quite a few years and it's worked out great. The service is on top of all the various requirements and they also provide Human Resources services (hiring, firing, what you're allowed to do with employees according to state and federal regulations). Much is happening with Human Resources these days regarding workplace discrimination, employee training and safety, employee recruiting and termination policies, and the essential employee handbook. The subject of employees is covered in Step Two, Operations.

It may cost you money to buy accounting software or use a payroll service, but believe me, the savings in time and stress is worth it.

### Loans and Lenders

If you're just starting out, it can be tough to get a loan. From the case studies presented later in the book, you can see just how many businesses started by putting in their own money or raising it from family and friends. I started my business with a government Small Business Administration (SBA) loan. I paid it off in two years, but it involved mountains of paperwork and took almost six months to get the funding.

One interesting note about SBA loans is that the Small Business Administration doesn't actually loan you the money; you have to apply at a bank. The SBA simply guarantees the bank repayment in the event you default.

### Your Credit Score

There are three agencies that collect and maintain information on your credit history: Equifax, Experian, and Trans Union. These agencies calculate your credit score, commonly known as your FICO score (an acronym for Fair Isaac Corporation). The five types of credit data that are used to determine your FICO score are payment history, amounts owed, length of credit history, new credit, and types of credit used. Lenders will obtain your credit rating from one or all of the above agencies. If you have any notable negative credit history, such as a tax lien, a lender may decline your request for a loan.

Here's one more thought regarding Finance: Hire an outside consultant. I have used one regularly every month for over a decade, not only with the financials, but with new business development strategies. An outside consultant will help you by providing an outsider's perspective.

Finally, I must repeat that since finance may not be your strong suit, don't neglect it. If you do, you may end up becoming just another statistic. According to the Small Business Administration, more than half of all small businesses fail within five years.

As for how much income the average small business brings in annually, below are some statistics from Janet Attard's website, www.businessknowhow.com.

## Average Income for Small Businesses

As you can see from the chart on the next page, only 10 percent of all small businesses have annual sales approaching $1 million. For those who reach this milestone, it can be a cause for celebration. If you exclude businesses earning under $25,000 a year, the average small business will have annual sales between $50,000 and $500,000.

My company finally reached the $1 million plateau after thirteen years in business. I framed a copy of the profit and loss statement that my bookkeeper prepared on the day we went over the million mark. It's on my credenza for all of my Little Biz clients to see and appreciate that it really can be done.

Don't let the chart below throw you. My belief is that many of those owners who have never passed $500,000 in annual sales haven't fully followed the "Five Steps to Your First Million." If you follow the steps that I've laid out here, you'll do it.

The Little Business Book Step Three - Finance

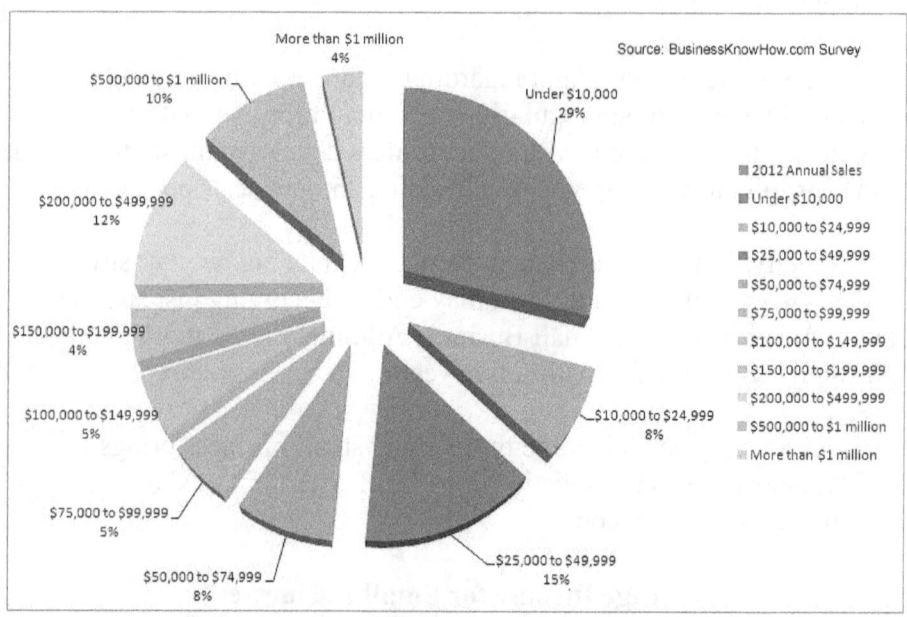

Source: Attard Communications, Inc. Reprinted with permission.

Next, here's my interview with an owner who bought an existing business that he had to start almost from scratch. Nothing is ever really what it seems.

**Category: Locksmith & Security**

When Scott Edelstein took this company over in 2001, it was struggling and it took more than a few twelve-hour days and lots of dedication to put it on a success track. Today, all that effort has paid off and Scott is now realizing the best gross revenues and net profits ever.

*AA Safe & Security is a security solutions provider specializing in card access systems, video surveillance, intercoms, doors and frames, ADA compliance, and a variety of the most sophisticated lock systems on the market. The company's latest financials show a 24% increase over last year.*

*Bye, bye recession? Maybe, but Scott knows not to get too comfortable because small businesses can be impacted by economic downturns when you least expect them.*

Year started (or took over) the business: *2001*
Amount of startup capital (either a loan or your own money): *$75,000*
Obtained startup capital from: *His own money*
Number of employees at startup: *3*   Number of employees today: *7*
Gross revenue first fiscal year: *$300,000*   Gross revenue last fiscal year: *$1.1 mil*
How many years did it take before you started making a satisfactory profit: *10*

Most valuable idea or action you've taken: *Changing the company name from locksmith to security opened many new doors. Changed the business model from strictly residential to much more commercial (due, in part, to the recession).*

Least valuable idea or action you've taken: *Shouldn't have closed my first store when I opened this business. I should be expanding into another geographic location.*
What's more important?

- The value of your services: *X*    Or    - The price of your services: _____

- Why? *Competitors can't bring the kind of value we offer. We're licensed and bonded with clean and beautiful vehicles and a gorgeous storefront.*

- Return customers: *X*        Or    - Advertising: _____

## The Little Business Book Step Three - Finance

> Why? *Return customers are the bulk of my business. Our strategy is to go after recurring business. We're constantly building great, long-term relationships.*

- Cash flow: _____         Or    - Credit rating: *X*

- Why? *A good credit rating allows me to get cash when I need it.*

- Understanding your financials *X*    Or   - Being good at what you do: _____

- Why? *Understanding your financials is essential to running a successful business. I always pay things off quickly, thus we rarely have much debt.*

Best advice for a new owner (or one who's not yet successful):

*Be patient – success doesn't happen overnight. Be sufficiently funded before you start. If you start with too little, you won't have cash flow and you won't be able to get a loan. Also, I'm a strong proponent of developing thorough systems and procedures. Most importantly, hire good people. Don't try to do it all yourself.*

*Additional thoughts: I was too involved <u>in</u> my business rather than <u>on</u> my business. In other words, you should spend less time acting like an employee and more time learning how to make a profit. Continue to reinvest in your business.*

*It takes a few years to become long-term successful. You must persevere. Regarding cash, peace of mind is phenomenal when you have cash. When there isn't enough cash, there isn't any peace of mind.*

*Do your homework. Is your new business really needed in your area? Ask yourself, "Why do I want to do this?" Hire employees who want to help your business grow. Then help your employees become successful.*

Here are the highlights of Step Three for your quick review.

## FINANCE HIGHLIGHTS

- Understanding financials doesn't require excellence in math.

- Prepare an estimate of all your expenses.

- Decide how much profit you want to make.

- Acquire a software program for accounting.

- Hire a bookkeeper and an accountant, if only on a limited basis.

- Learn to read and understand your profit and loss statement.

- Prepare a weekly cash flow statement.

- Set monthly goals for how much income you expect to receive.

- Prepare a 12-month budget that projects future income and expenses.

- For payroll, use your accounting software or a payroll service.

# Step Four

# Marketing & Sales

**Wherein you learn to build a targeted, loyal clientele who will come back to you regularly.**

We've finally reached the subject of selling your products or services. That's why you're in business to begin with, right? It's time to make some money and in this step you're going to do exactly that.

### What's the difference between marketing and sales?

You often hear this segment of business referred to as Sales and Marketing, but you actually have to do the marketing first before you can do the sales. What's the difference between the two?

*Marketing is reviewing the entire landscape of potential customers and then deciding which categories of customers you want to target.*

*Sales is working with an individual customer.*

Starting with Marketing, how do you select your potential customers? My long-time friend and business advisor, Bill Ross, suggested using the chart below to illustrate how the selection process and proposal works.

Let's break down this inverted marketing pyramid to see how you ultimately get to your actual customer and make a sale.

1. Start with all potential customers.

    In some cases, this could mean the whole world, but most likely, depending on your product or service, this would be your geographic service area. Are your customers going to come from just your neighborhood, your town, or your county or state?

    What customer categories will your product or service appeal to – high-end residential, businesses, seniors, sports fans, health enthusiasts, etc.? Begin by identifying anyone who might benefit from your product or service. The value in this overview selection process lies in who you are able to eliminate from this list. I know, you believe your idea is so spectacular that it would benefit everyone, but let's get realistic; there are a few folks who simply won't be interested. Get them off the list. Unless you're strictly an online business, why don't you just start with your town? That would be realistic.

2. Next, select realistic prospects.

    This is where you shift into target marketing. Here's where you define very specific customer categories. Now you're going to limit your choices considerably and eliminate many potential customers from the list. We don't want you wasting valuable time and money on disinterested prospects, so be very discriminating here. If you were to go out and make a sales presentation right now, who would actually buy – and why?

The next four items on the pyramid are part of the Sales process, which we'll get to shortly. For now, let's stay with Marketing. When most people think of Marketing, they assume it means Advertising. Marketing involves a lot more than just putting an ad in the paper.

The following list, The Top Forty Marketing Tools, will give you a good overview of all the options at your disposal for getting the word out about your product or service. Most of the business owners I interviewed for the case studies included in the appendix of this book have likely tried all forty of them.

The revelation here is that there isn't just one marketing technique that works for small businesses. At a minimum, you will need to utilize at least a half-dozen items from the Top Forty list, used consistently and repeatedly, to have success with your marketing. One of the nice things about being a small-business owner with an even smaller marketing budget is that we get to be creative, something the big boys can't do without a humongous ad budget.

### The Top Forty Marketing Tools

 = Best Bets

1. Logo design ★

    Logo design begins with your identifier – in print, on a business card, or a web page. Your graphic imprint sets up an immediate emotional response. It tells your customers in a millisecond whether you're smart, creative, and professional or just a copycat, indistinguishable from all the rest.

    You can do the logo design yourself or you can hire a graphic artist. Your logo is the simplest and quickest way to establish your standards. It can be a symbol, a photo, or an unusual font used for your business name. Unless you're Hewlett-Packard, it's probably not a good idea to use just capital letters like CB or JAO, that's meaningless. Spend some time on this one – the logo is going to go on everything, business cards, letterhead, web page, contracts, print advertising, TV ads and vehicle signs. [WEB SEARCH; Company logo design]

2. Business Cards

    Business cards are universal introductions that really provide just one thing: contact information. Don't go nuts with these things. You can get them really cheap online. Business cards don't close deals or motivate purchases. They're just the equivalent of an introduction. Nothing else happens with business cards unless you want to magnetize them for use on your customer's refrigerator door (in my experience, not a successful marketing tool).

3. Brochures

   Many businesses spend a lot of money on fancy four-color brochures. No need to do that anymore. Now you can print them on your office printer, although I don't do that; it takes too much time and the heavier card stock isn't cheap. Brochures are a misguided venture into sales. They don't sell; they're not deal closers. You, in person, are the deal closer. Because brochures are larger than business cards, they give you more room to feature what you do, but if you consider how much print, photo, and video space is available on your website, brochures can't feature all of that. I still use brochures, and in the past, I would reorder them regularly, but I can't remember the last time I reordered a thousand brochures.

4. Web Pages & Social Media ★

   This is where the action is today, but who knows what's coming vis-à-vis computers and smartphones. Consider taking mini-courses on how to use Linked In, Facebook, and Twitter. I believe social media can be an important marketing tool, but you may need to hire someone to manage it. I designed our website and found the process to be fun and creative. You don't need to be that computer savvy; most of these programs are simple enough for a fifth grader. You can also hire this out, for a price, but think about giving it a shot yourself. There are all kinds of website builder programs available now at very reasonable prices; check weebly.com, wix.com, and squarespace.com. Web page designers will also register your domain name and get you up and running online in a snap. [WEB SEARCH: Web builders]

Most consumers access the web regularly instead of that old dinosaur, the yellow pages. Your yellow page presence should be just a one-line entry with your phone number. If you must make it larger, don't do anything more than a 1-inch display ad and include your logo. Dollar for dollar, I believe your web page will yield a better return.

5. Blogs

   Blogs are one of the oldest ways of carrying on conversations on the web. There are a number of sites that can host a blog for you (e.g., Google owns a site called Blogger.com). You can either create your own stand-alone blog on the web or attach it to your existing website. Through your blog, you can bring customers up to speed on your latest products and services and get customer reviews, but blog use is preferred for creating a forum where folks can offer helpful information. If you add a blog to your marketing strategy, you may hear from some people who believe blogs should be used only be for non-commercial purposes, but that's just not so. Blogs come in both free and paid versions. [WEB SEARCH: How to build a blog]

6. Website Videos

   One advantage the web has over print media is that you can include videos on your site. If you have a GoPro camera and you're in forest management, you can show customers your view of the forest from the top of the highest redwood. If you sell eyewear, you can show them how transition lenses work. The opportunities for video display are endless.

7. T-shirts, Branded Clothing and Uniforms ★

   I've long been a fan of uniforms with your logo on them. Right off the bat, ask your employees to help you pick the style of their uniforms. T-shirts with your logo are great to give out to customers.

8. Customer Reviews, Testimonials, and Surveys ★

    I believe people read reviews, and Angie's List is a good site. I can't tell you how much potential business you lose from a bad review. Do whatever it takes, including customer refunds, to stay in the five-star range, because a bad review will stick to you worse than a bad habit. That's just the way it is nowdays. Also, consider becoming a Better Business Bureau member. Many customers check BBB reviews.

    Regarding testimonials: ask your customers for a letter of recommendation and feature these on your website. Also, think about doing an annual survey of your existing customers; they'll appreciate the opportunity for input.

9. Volunteer Work ★

    If you want to give back to the community, then get out there and help. That's another benefit of being a small business. You know what the community needs. Get involved. It will further your vision and help your community. It doesn't take much. For example, every year we install Christmas lights for our local downtown area.

10. Email

    You use email all the time, but can this be another marketing tool? Maybe. Start by reminding yourself of all the spam, sales pitches, and other garbage email you dump in the trash every day. If you don't want to be one of those time-wasters, then you must have a very specific reason to use email for marketing purposes. First, ask yourself if this is something your email recipients absolutely need to know. Second, keep it short – no more than three sentences. Screenwriters have to grab their audience in the first ten pages. If songwriters can't tell a familiar story in 2 minutes and 45 seconds, forget it. You do not make sales with email. You'll be lucky if you can even get an appointment using email. You should just use email for thank-you's.

11. Postcards

    I've tried them. I've sent them to a specific block in a highly researched (home prices, estimated income range) neighborhood. I've sent them to the same select neighborhoods three times in a row, one month apart with no results.

12. Flyers

    Flyers are a hybrid mix of business cards and brochures. They don't sell anything, but they can be useful with your existing clients to highlight future promotions. I once had a novice salesperson who was going to head up our booth at an outdoor event. She insisted on preparing a lengthy flyer announcing all the wonderful things we do. I told her that wordy documents usually go unread. She agreed to edit it down but ultimately came back with even more verbiage. I let her have her way. We didn't sell anything that day. You're the one who does the selling, not flyers or brochures, pens or coffee cups. We'll get into that more in the section on Sales.

13. Door Hangers

    This is a judgment call. What impression does the average person get of your company when they find one of these hanging on their front doorknob? If it turns out that coincidentally they happen to need your product or service right then, maybe you'll make a sale. I've used them on occasion in the neighborhood surrounding a client for whom we happened to working that day.

14. Newspapers ★

    Many small businesses advertise in their local newspapers regularly, possibly because it's been the method of choice for many years. But "the times they are a-changin." For many businesses, the newspaper is the only advertising source they use, and as long as they see a regular return on their investment, they may not need anything else. Supermarkets and drugstores rely heavily on their weekly ads and inserts, as do restaurants. The important word is "regularly".

If you spend $1,000 for one newspaper ad to run only once, and the return on investment is low, it may shake your confidence in such media. As with radio and TV, you have to do it a lot! Readers have to get used to seeing your logo regularly and maybe they might actually read your ad. Repetition breeds familiarity. Since there are thousands of businesses that use the newspaper, you should consider it, but not on a one-time basis.

### 15. Press Releases ★

The term "PR" has been around for ages, and there is some value in using it. Since press releases in your local newspapers or trade journals are usually free, it's a no-cost way to get your name out there. You will need to contact the newspaper or journal and find out what their PR format is. They'll tell you exactly what they will accept, and they won't guarantee that they'll print whatever you send them. Your full press release may be edited down to only a few paragraphs, but nonetheless, it's free, so why not?

### 16. Local Magazines ★

This is a more folksy approach to attracting new business because it's locally focused. You could try a one-time shot with a local magazine. Realtors like them (full-page, four-color) and so do charity events.

### 17. Newsletters

Newsletters have some validity. They can be useful for dispensing topical and timely information, but they're definitely not a deal-closer. In addition, you better have a dedicated employee who's willing to crank out a newsletter once a month, every month. Maybe try a once-a-year newsletter – but not at Christmas.

### 18. Phone On-Hold Messages

These are easy to do. Most phone systems allow you to record a voice intro, and you can even spend extra time adding music. I think the music defines you more than what you're saying.

19. Building Signage, Store Windows and Office Interiors ★

The amount of money you spend on building or office signs depends, in part, on whether or not you have a lot of retail traffic. It's obvious that retail businesses spend a considerable amount on signs and store windows because it's an open invitation to cross their threshold. On the other hand, office interiors are somewhat dependent on how important the person behind the desk thinks he or she is. At the very least, get comfortable chairs.

20. Vehicle Signage and Ad-Wraps, Vehicle Appearance ★

Car, truck, and van signs are free advertising and are potentially seen by thousands of people during the day. However, one important note for your employees: your company name and phone number is a flashing neon sign if the driver is speeding, driving aggressively, or flipping people off. (I actually got a call about one of our guys, and that doesn't help business or public relations.)

Vehicle wraps aren't cheap, but they sure look beautiful. Go with something that looks professional and make the phone number large enough to be seen in the flash of an eye. Personally, I've never cared for the magnetic door signs on automobiles, but they might be workable for larger vehicles. Check out whether your state Department of Motor Vehicles requires motor-carrier or contractor numbers on business vehicles.

It goes without saying that your vehicles should be kept clean, regularly, especially for a first appointment or a sales call. First impressions make a difference.

21. Nonprofit 501c(3) for Community Outreach ★

One area of marketing that many businesses are often unaware of is setting up a separate nonprofit company that uses your existing company name with the word "foundation" appended to it, for example, The Discovery Gardens Foundation, a 501c(3).

Creating a nonprofit foundation allows you to hold events and raise money for your favorite community organizations without having to pay taxes on the money you raise. Our foundation raises funds for music and art programs in local schools. The advantage for a small business is that it's another way of getting your name out there. You file for 501c(3) status with the IRS and it can take six months to get approved.

22. Gift Certificates

    You may want to offer gift certificates, but they may be of limited marketing value. Possibly they could bring some word-of-mouth referrals.

23. Recreational and Religious Facilities

    Share your business offerings with members of your church and recreational sports or health clubs, but don't be too aggressive. Too much chitchat about your business can be a real turn-off, especially on the golf course. You might want to erect a sign on the Little League fence, but make it readable from 300 feet.

24. Charity Events and Auctions ★

    This is another opportunity for community interaction and can be another valuable advantage for small businesses. You need to be realistic about what kind of financial return you'll get from such events, so don't go overboard with your budget.

25. Chamber of Commerce Mixers

    I no longer attend these though I know there are those who will vigorously argue that I'm wrong. It seems that mixers are just an opportunity to exchange business cards. I've never closed a deal at one.

26. Sports Team Sponsorship

    There's not much financial return in having your business name on sports team uniforms, but the value lies in your opportunity to take a break and enjoy the kids and the game. Destressing has value because it helps you relax and get your head clear. Maybe you'll come back to work with a fresh approach to your marketing.

27. Direct Mail

In spite of the fact that a business owner may expect a 20% return on his mailing, the average return is closer to 2%. The best interaction with a potential customer is always face-to-face. Direct mail doesn't offer a good return on your investment or your time.
[WEB SEARCH: Average return on direct mail]

28. Radio and TV Advertisement

Try advertising on both Radio and TV even though it is costly. You will need to commit to a sufficient number of spots because a one-time ad won't do anything for you. Remember, familiarity breeds repetition.

Radio and TV salespeople will present their demographics (age of listeners, etc.), and reach (how many people receive their station's signal), and ratings (percentage of the total audience that listens to them).

This may make no sense to you, but a number of local businesses say they get *some* value from this kind of advertising. Remember, you have to regularly use at least half a dozen items from this Top Forty list; just trying one thing, like radio and TV, is not going to effective. Therefore, don't spend your entire year's advertising budget on a big buy for morning-drive or evening-news times.

29. Contest Sponsorship

Sponsoring a contest can give you a valid reason for advertising in the newspaper or radio. Consider sponsoring a photo contest or a children's art competition, or even a surfing or skiing contest or a marathon, depending on your location.

30. Seminars and Speaking Engagements

These can be valuable ways of displaying your expertise, but they take time to prepare. If you're not a confident speaker, find someone in your organization who could do it. You'll likely get some customers and possibly even potential employees.

31. Books, E-books and Magazine Articles

If you're an expert in the field of your product or service, consider writing a book or submitting magazine articles. The cost of self-publishing a book is reasonable and authoring magazine articles gets your name out there. Adobe offers InDesign software that will prepare your manuscript for both print and E-books. [WEB SEARCH: Self publishing]

32. Annual Sale

Some businesses do very well having an annual sale, investing most of their advertising budget at one particular time of year. If you do this regularly, customers will get used to looking for it, and you will probably get a decent and predictable response. However, don't give away the shop just to produce bodies. If you lose money on 200 low-ball, price-conscious customers, you just lose money.

33. Event and Trade Show Displays

Again, kind of a tough call. We've done them. They take a considerable amount of preparation time, and such booths don't go for cheap. You can expect to see the bigger players in your community at these events; this is the place for real pitchmen. If you're not one of those, you probably won't do more than one of these (but you might try at least one).

34. Specialty Products Branded for Hand-outs

This is *not* the business we should all go into to make big bucks. Such ventures net utterly worthless garbage headed for the trash bin. It won't add a dime to your bottom line. However, and this is a big however, your existing customers might like to have one of your t-shirts or something else of real value, but they won't buy more of your products or services because of it.

### 35. Point-of-Sale Displays

There's value here, particularly in a retail location and possibly at trade shows. Get your displays done professionally; the do-it-yourself ones look amateurish. Even the best displays age with time. You can't reuse them forever.

### 36. Business and Trade Publications

You might be able to do some marketing using trade publications, but you may have better luck with them if they are used as a source for employment. I get stacks of these publications in the mail; sometimes they have really helpful articles regarding your particular trade.

### 37. Coupons

When we first opened our business, mailing coupons for either 20% off or $100 off became our first official crutch. After two years, I did a calculation of who our coupon customers were – nothing but bottom feeders. For a $200 job, they wanted to use the $100 off coupon. That wouldn't even cover our job cost.

### 38. Memorable or Toll-free Phone Numbers

You should have an 800 number for customers outside of your area code. Use it in all your advertising, including letterhead and business cards.

A memorable number that converts to letters such as 800 456-8396, which is also 800 I LOVE YOU, may make it easier for customers to remember you.

### 39. Adopt-a-Highway Signs

These are really more of a community service than a client-builder. Actually, they're hard to get; we were on a waiting list for over a year and never got one. You can try for a particular highway location, but the good ones are probably all taken. You have to regularly police the area around your sign for trash, sometimes up to a mile, though you can hire an outside company to do this for you. However, the cost varies and the signs are subject to vandalism.

40. Yellow Pages

You may consider it necessary to put an ad in the yellow pages if only to make your contact information available. However, it can be expensive to buy a half or full-page ad. More customers may search for you on the Internet.

Okay, now that we've made it through the Top Forty, I have to issue a disclaimer. While I've personally used most of the methods listed above and gotten the responses that I've indicated, I don't think there is a soul out there who can tell you exactly what to do or what not to do. Some will say, "Hey, newspaper advertising works great for me" or "Chamber mixers are the best" or "I always get a 20% return on postcards." However, when you're working with a small marketing budget, you can't try everything you'd like to try.

We once bought a page in the local golf course guide for a year. One year passed and . . . nothing. Not even one call. Then, for six months, we tried advertisements on the back of a large grocery chain's customer receipts, to be seen by thousands of people. Six months passed and . . . nothing.

There is no one single way to market your business.

## The Most Important Ingredients in the Sales Process

Your approach to sales must provide a truly invigorating experience for every one of your clients and must give them the kind of value they don't expect from other companies. You already know that client-centered service is aimed at establishing a rock-solid level of trust and understanding which will account for a large number of return clients and allow you to maintain your target goals in terms of revenue.

In the following pages, you will find a detailed breakdown of the sales process, beginning with an overview of the elements shown in the marketing pyramid that are necessary to not only close the sale but establish a long-term relationship with your clients. Inherent in these elements is the high priority of understanding your clients' business needs and then building an unshakeable trust in your products or services that has them continually returning to you.

To appreciate your clients' needs, which are similar to those of most buyers of any goods and services throughout the country, we'll focus on basic motivations such as trust, credibility, relationship, and value. But first, consider my overall approach to Sales below.

The complexity of the selling process has been documented in countless books and seminars, but most of these don't emphasize the basic simplicity of human interaction – sharing your passion for the work you do or the product you produce and reinforcing it with the years of experience that invigorate this spirit. Your passion is an important ingredient in the selling process.

I emphasize the simple act of listening, a very important element of communication. Rattling off a list of reasons the client should buy from you is not only the quickest way to turn someone off, it's also the mark of a novice. In the following pages you'll learn how to ask and answer questions, how to listen and qualify your clients to determine if they have a genuine interest in your product or service and for you to understand and appreciate the full scope of their needs.

Next – the remaining elements in the marketing pyramid.

### Overview of Sales Elements

**I.      The Initial Presentation**
- Build rapport

- Earn trust
- Establish equality between you and your client
- Determine need
- Establish credibility
- Qualify (1$^{st}$ time)

(Note: *Qualifying* means determining, by various observations, whether the customer you are working with may ultimately become a buyer of your product or service.)

**II.   The Analysis of Needs**
- Appreciate your clients' logical and emotional needs
- Listen
- Ask specific questions
- Begin setting the stage for a proposal
- Qualify (2$^{nd}$ time)

**III.   The Proposal**
- Present your solutions
- Appreciate their objections
- Revalidate their needs, both logical and emotional
- Qualify (3$^{rd}$ and final time

**IV.   The Agreement**
- Provide validation and proof of reputation
- Review payment policy
- Have client sign estimate/contract
- Schedule the work or deliver the product
- Follow up to get client input
- Ask for reviews and referrals
- Manage continuing relationship

*Note: the above is a brief overview. A more detailed explanation is shown on Page 72, The Sales Process In Depth.*

## Build your Foundation on the Basic Motivations

TRUST – CREDIBILITY – RELATIONSHIP – VALUE

### *Building Trust*

Key elements:

- Be punctual or call if you're going to be late.
- Don't promise what you can't deliver.
- Make no promises other than those you can fulfill.
- Emphasize your knowledge and that of your staff.
- Inform the client of your Guarantee of Quality (see Step Five – Service).

A few more ways to build trust:

- Always stand by your word.
- Always follow through on what you've promised.
- Be honest and forthright with your factual knowledge of your competitors' products or services, but never be negative or derogatory. It's okay to inform your clients of your competitor's *deficiencies*, but you better be correct and you must be able to prove it.
- Listen and give helpful answers; never dictate.
- Give specific responses that offer *valuable* information.
- For any question you can't answer, check further and respond to them the same day.

### *Building Credibility*

Key elements:

- Explain your qualifications.
- Note your length of time in business.
- Give them proof that your business meets all legal requirements.

More ways to build credibility:

- At first meeting, present a business card, a brochure and your Guarantee of Quality card.
- Give them references of satisfied clients.
- Suggest they visit your website and view your many letters of recommendation.

## *Building Relationship*

Key elements:

- Become simpatico; enjoy being in their company.
- Explore the human value of client friendship.
- Listen to what they're saying.
- Offer helpful and timely solutions.

More ways to build relationship:

- When you respect them as a client, they will respect you for your professionalism and knowledge.
- You're providing them with the best from the best.
- Discover what you have in common.
- Brainstorm with them; they'll enjoy it.
- ***Building Value***

Key elements:

- Give a timely response to their request.

- Obtain a clear understanding of their need and then rephrase and repeat back to them to make sure you understood them correctly.
- Provide a satisfying and memorable conclusion to their experience.
- Follow up to get their feelings about your product or service.

More ways to demonstrate value:

- Tell them you're fully insured.
- Tell them you offer ongoing education programs for your employees.
- Tell them you practice the most recent industry standards.
- Tell them about your community involvement.
- And finally – need I say it again – Listen!

### How To Ask Questions

Below are some basic ways to ask questions of your clients.

**What does your client want?**

*"Besides what we're talking about now, is there anything else you'd like?"*

**What does your client expect from you?**

*"What do you want to get from my product or service?"*

**What is your client's time frame?**

*"Do you have a specific date or time in mind?"*

**Has your client ever had problems with this kind of product or service in the past?**

*"What has been your past experience with this?"*

**Does your client know how to maintain your product or service?**

*"Can I give you any further tips on how to handle this once we're done?"*

**Is your client a candidate for future offers you may provide?**

*"May I tell you about something that's coming up in the future?"*

### How To Answer Questions

Below are some suggested responses to questions.

**How much does it cost?**

*"Our price is determined not only by the quality of our service or product but also by what it costs us to provide it."*

**How much do you charge per hour?**

*"We don't charge by the hour. We price each item of service individually."*

**I'm just looking. I'll let you know if I'm interested.**

*"Is price the primary consideration for you?"*

### What You Don't Do

It's important to minimize your talking. Spend at least 75 percent of your time listening. If your client needs more assistance to help them make a decision, refrain from giving them a mile-long list of what you do. Instead, tell them what you *don't* do:

- We don't price our product or service without describing exactly what it comprises.
- We don't work without permits.
- We don't offer service that we are not professionally trained to do.
- We don't hire unqualified employees.
- We don't use unsafe vehicles or substandard equipment.

### Selling Value Over Price

For the last 50 years or more, Americans have pursued a habit which today is fully ingrained in shopping – looking for products and services that are "On Sale." Most retailers feature items that suggest they are "better and cheaper" than those of their competitors using come-ons such as "10% Off," "2 for 1," "Free Shipping," and "But wait, there's more." Cheaper is rarely better, yet we are all led to believe we can buy cheaper products and services and actually be satisfied with them. However, our satisfaction may derive from priding ourselves on knowing how to find the "best deal," rather than from the product or service itself.

Continually accepting things of lesser value is part of the sales game we've become accustomed to: you pay less, you get less, and then you repeat the cycle all over again. Because "finding deals" is the norm, we think we're content with the results and getting products and services that offer real value becomes secondary.

Because your product or service should be based on value and not price, you have a real hill to climb not only with your clients but with yourself. Every time you come home from the mall and tell someone that you got something "on sale," you reinforce the idea that this is the normal and preferred way to buy things. American consumers may never change that style. Therefore, how do you convince your clients that your company offers something better than "price?"

We will pay for value if we understand and appreciate the nature of the value. Selling your product or service cheaply doesn't necessarily reflect its value. There are times when something of real value goes on sale, but if you always sell cheap, what is your customer's underlying expectation? Do they really believe they're going to be satisfied by your bargain deal? Possibly for the next 3 minutes, but after that they're back to looking for another deal and they'll lump you and ten of your competitors together in the process. Will they come back to you again? Who knows?

Ultimately, regarding selling value over price, inherent in your sales process is the high priority of understanding your clients' business needs as well as their emotional motivations and then building an unshakeable trust in the value of your product or service that has them continually returning to you over the long haul. Some clients may rightfully, and out of necessity, buy based on price. However, don't dismiss your client's unseen *emotional* needs or you might miss their underlying motivation.

Keeping in mind that it all begins with value, not price, how do you engage with your clients? Of course, they're entitled to great service; now here are the important elements of sales.

## The Sales Process In Depth

### *The Initial Meeting or Presentation*

#### Build Rapport

Begin your meeting or presentation by building rapport. Rapport, from the French word *rapporter*, means "to bring back", an apt description of your first meeting which starts by offering a relationship that seeks harmony and a sense of simpatico. Kind of like the days when folks frequented their neighborhood shops because they liked the owners and trusted them. This is your first opportunity to establish a long-term relationship.

### Earn Trust

To build rapport, you need to earn your client's trust right from the start. Hand them your Guarantee of Quality card and tell them that your reputation (and your bank account) is on the line with every job you do. Tell them that they, and all your clients, are the reason your business grows every year. You do good work and they can trust your expertise because of the knowledge you have and the value you offer. They must recognize that you give value because you are valuable.

### Establish Equality Between You and Your Client

You need to guide your clients to a place where they know their input and expectations are important. Start by creating a mutual goal, an equal pairing of energies seeking the same result.

Use Active Listening. This is where you are making a conscious effort to understand and appreciate what they are saying instead of mentally preparing your answer before they've finished speaking.

### Determine Need

It's not unusual when clients call that there may be more "there" than meets the eye. Your average client may be well informed and sophisticated, but rarely do they possess your wealth of product or service knowledge. You're the pro and you're the one who should determine the best solution for their needs. Ask questions and listen closely to their answers. Repeat their stated needs back to them.

### Establish Credibility

Your clients should access your website and the letters of recommendation exhibited. They should read reviews of your business on Angie's List or the Better Business Bureau. Possibly they have friends who were delighted with your work.

Note your professional credentials but don't bend their ear incessantly. Get to the point, state the facts, and move on. If they're cautious, that's all right. You will ultimately replace any lingering skepticism with an anticipation of genuine value.

### Qualify (1st Time)

The need to qualify appears at three different times during your presentation. This first one deals with just the facts. My experience shows that the Achilles' heel of all sales presentations is the owner's inability to adequately qualify the client. Qualifying means making the assessment that this client may become a buyer of your product or service rather than learning at the end of your presentation that they were never a candidate to begin with.

Not all prospects make good clients. At this early stage of your presentation, you must determine if your client is a good fit. If not, let them go quickly. The most important questions you should ask are: Why did they come to you? Have they gotten any other quotes? Will they automatically go with the lowest quote because their primary interest is price?

## *The Analysis of Needs*

### Appreciate Both Their Logical and Emotional Needs

Some buying decisions are based on a combination of both logical and emotional needs. A purely logical purchase would be refueling your car or paying your monthly power bill. In some situations, there may be an element of emotion involved as well.

Don't lose sight of the fact that your client may not be focused only on price. Emotional decision-making isn't always visible in your clients' responses. (Think about the last time you bought a car; did you tell the salesperson you really wanted that car? Or did you shift into a "take-it-or-leave-it" attitude as a negotiating tactic?) Determine what else there is besides "How much?"

How do you begin to appreciate your clients' emotional needs?

**Listen**

Make sure you're in total listening mode before you even shake hands. Listen for their apprehension, frustration, and expectations. Your mind should be focused not only on this sale but on the next one when they call you to hire you again. You have the right answer – that's within the very nature of your business. But if you haven't fully heard them out, you'll have the wrong answer.

**Ask Specific Questions**

You're in front of your client to deliver a specific product or service and provide them with your professional expertise. Your questions should be directed toward determining their logical and emotional needs, and your answers should inform and educate them in ways they may not get from your competitors.

Make sure your questions and the resulting answers are crystal clear and not subject to misinterpretation. Have you overlooked anything? Has your client disclosed everything? Will the product or service be as planned and agreed?

**Begin Setting the Stage for a Proposal**

Review with your client the initial conclusions you've drawn based on what you've observed and their answers to your questions. At this stage, present a menu of alternatives, beginning with the most pain-free (price-wise and time-wise) and ending with your recommendation for completing the job to their satisfaction.

This is the "test-the-waters" moment where you analyze your client's response to the initial options you've presented. Their response will reveal whether you've missed something in the prior steps of your presentation. At this stage, you're nearing the halfway point of your presentation and the next step will determine whether you should continue or call it a day.

## Qualify (2nd Time)

First, summarize and review what your client has told you. Then listen to any concerns they may have. Sometimes at this stage, your client may say they've gotten a cheaper quote elsewhere. This is where we encounter the most common *"apples vs. oranges"* perception. The competing quote rarely addresses the value of what you are proposing. To make a legitimate comparison, you must ask the details of the other quote and explain how it differs from yours.

Try to determine if the other quote is the result of a friend or a neighbor's referral. Maybe their club or organization always uses the other business. Ask your client if they are concerned about the quality of the other company. Their answer should quickly tell you if they are fixated on price. Explain the added value of your proposal and the potential drawbacks of your competitor's offering.

## The Proposal

### Present Your Solutions

On the basis of your mutual disclosures, you can now decide what you can do to assure a high-value result. Explain your reasoning clearly, giving particular emphasis to the resulting value to be achieved. You may want to point to successes you've had in the past in a similar situation.

### Appreciate Their Objections

Your client should now feel comfortable enough to share any remaining concerns with you. In all likelihood, they want you to help them say "yes." Otherwise, you would have already determined (during the previous qualifying stages) that their objections were aimed at getting you to lower your price.

If they have concerns that you can't address on the spot, tell them you'll have answers for them quickly. And get back to them that same day if you can.

### Revalidate Their Needs, both Logical and Emotional

Take your client back to the original reason they came to you. Review their original request and ask if you have satisfied all of their concerns. Restate the reasons that you are proposing your product or your particular service and make sure they understand and appreciate the value of your proposal.

### Qualify (3rd and Final Time)

Is your client ready to go forward? Are they satisfied with the price? Is there anyone else who must approve before the transaction can be completed?

This is your last opportunity to assess a good fit between you and your client. Make sure you've covered all the bases before you move on to the agreement.

## *The Agreement*

### Provide Validation and Proof of Reputation

You might provide a potential client with photos or videos. Also, if you're performing a service, provide them with a copy of your General liability insurance policy and name them as an Additional Insured if they wish. They may also request evidence of Workers Compensation coverage and you should provide them with this.

### Review Payment Policy

Tell them what your preferred payment method is: cash, check, or credit card. I don't recommend that you offer an extended payment plan because this will have a direct effect on your cash flow. Many clients prefer to use a credit card and you should honor these requests, even though it will incur a 1% to 3% service charge. It is important that you clarify your preferred method of payment at the time you complete the agreement. Don't leave the question of payment method to chance just so you can appear to be nonchalant about it.

While the contract signer bears responsibility for payment, if someone else will be paying, get contact information for that party. A typical example of this is when the son signs the contract for work to be done at his mother's house. Your contract should include the General Contract Conditions prepared by you or your attorney that protect you in the event of a dispute or default.

### Have Client Sign Estimate/Contract

You'd be surprised how many new salespeople fear this point in their presentation. Any hesitation on your part will probably result in the loss of the sale. Just know that you are valuable and that your client trusts you.

### Scheduling and Delivery

Schedule the work or deliver the product using your timeframe since your company must run like a well-oiled machine. But you must also place a premium on your client's request for a timely response. When you deliver your product or service, do so with pride in meeting your client's expectations.

### Follow Up To Get Client Input

Several days after the transaction is complete, call your client to make sure they are completely satisfied. Keep notes of their answers on file and share them with your employees. If there are any problems, handle them immediately.

### Ask for Reviews and Referrals

Ask your clients if they would be willing to mail (or email) you a letter of recommendation and post it on your website with their permission. With all satisfied clients, always request that they refer you to their friends and neighbors.

## Manage Continuing Relationship

The key to keeping clients returning well into the future lies in the management of your continuing relationship with them. Stay in touch with a phone call on a regular basis, maybe every six months. You'll want to track this with whatever program or calendar you use.

One last thought: We've talked about avoiding needless chitchat and getting right to the point, but don't misinterpret the meaning of "needless chitchat." Part of promoting simpatico is to engage in heartfelt communication that improves the quality of the experience you and your client have. This goes directly to the heart of any consideration of logical and *emotional* needs. Put yourself *emotionally* on the same page as your client and the resulting business arrangements will ensure that you will have made a loyal friend and customer for the life of your business. This, supported by the value of your product or service, is the best value of all.

## A Final Word about Words

To use or not to use, that is the question. Make a list of the most common words you see in advertising – 20% off, deep discount, free installation, all you can eat, order now, anniversary sale, big savings, affordable, free. Vow never to use these "invisible" words again.

"Free" is a four-letter word. Avoid it like the plague. Nothing is truly free. Someone, probably you, is going to pay. Are you rolling in so much dough that you can give anything away for free? Go through your local newspaper ads, make notes from TV, look for these overused words and cross them off your usability list forever.

Here's an interview with a different kind of business. It's literally out in the woods.

The Little Business Book Step Four – Marketing & Sales

**Category: Destination Resort Campground**

*Andrew Townsend is the Summer Camp Director for Kennolyn Camps and he's been with this fabulous forest experience for over twenty years. Andrew oversees the administrative side of this international summer camp which includes hiring and training staff, organizing food service and transportation, summer camp programs, handling insurance and scheduling equipment maintenance. He said at times he feels like the mayor of a little city. The camp was founded in 1946 and named after the founder's children, Ken and Carolyn.*

Year started (or took over) the business: *1946 - Andrew came on board 1993*
Amount of startup capital: *Founders - $10,000 in 1946*
Obtained major capital from: *$1.5 million FEMA loan after 1989 earthquake*
Number of employees at startup: *9*   Number of employees today: *17 full/140 part*
Gross revenue first fiscal year: *$4,500*   Gross revenue last fiscal year: *$2 million*
How many years did it take before you started making a <u>satisfactory</u> profit: *8*

Most valuable idea or action you've taken: *Consolidating what used to be separate high school and grade school camps into one location and using the other location as a day camp.*

Least valuable idea or action you've taken: *We tried to start an off-site travel program going to destinations as far away as Europe, but the kids like being here more than anywhere else.*

## The Little Business Book Step Four – Marketing & Sales

What's more important?

- The value of your services: ____    Or    - The price of your services: _X_

- Why? *Our price is not affected so much by our costs. We're selling an experience.*

- Return customers: _X_    Or    - Advertising: ____

- Why? *80% of our new business is word of mouth. We can't convey the atmosphere here through advertising.*

- Cash flow: _X_    Or    - Credit rating: ____

- Why? *We don't need credit. We take in most of our income in the spring and spend most of it in the summer.*

- Understanding your financials ____    Or    - Being good at what you do: _X_

- Why? *Without being good at what you do, there's no financials to worry about.*

Best advice for a new owner (or one who's not yet successful):

*Bring passion to what you do. Play to your strengths. Understand why this business fits you. Before you start, take a personal inventory. Ask yourself, "What am I really excited about?"*

Here are the highlights of Step Four for your quick review.

### MARKETING & SALES HIGHLIGHTS

- Use the potential customers chart to select realistic prospects.

- Use at least 6 items with a star from the Top Forty Marketing Tools.

- Qualify your prospects at least 3 times during the sales process.

- Listen more, talk less.

- Focus on building trust, credibility, relationship, and value.

- Tell your customers what you don't do.

- Ask specific questions, give specific answers. Avoid irrelevant chitchat.

- State your payment policy clearly.

- Ask for referrals and letters of recommendation.

- Follow up to determine if your customers are satisfied.

## Step Five

# Customer Service

**Wherein you learn the most important rule . . .
Always keep your customers happy.**

You've reached the final step and it's the most important one. When your customer service exceeds that of all your competitors, you will be on the path to a long and prosperous career as a small business owner.

### It's not about price, it's about value

Over the years, many books filled with tips and tricks and various grand schemes trumpeting the benefits of customer service have been proffered to the business community, mainly marketing departments of entities that we think of as big business, though you've probably bought a few of them yourself.

Rarely if ever does one find among this clambake of treasures real answers that might actually satisfy the American consumer, because these pearls of wisdom are cooked up for customers of companies with six-figure advertising budgets instead of real-world customers. Even the term "customer service" has lost any semblance of meaning because all companies, big and small, use it constantly, even though the actual service the customer receives is minimal. Let's analyze the words "customer service." For big business, the customers aren't really *their* customers; their customers are, in fact, their stockholders. The "customer service" they offer isn't how well their products perform; it's what kind of return their stockholders get on their investment.

That's an advantage for small business because your customers really *are* your customers. They can pick up the phone and call you directly. They don't have to talk to some call center in St. Louis first.

But ask any small business owner what their customer service is and you might get the catch-all response, "We're the best." Ask them how many customers come back again and again. Many small businesses don't even track those kinds of stats. Why? Because they don't realize how important customer service is. Instead, they think they're the best because of what I call "yada," some ethereal concept that nobody else knows how to measure except them.

They might tell you that this yada is described in their Mission Statement. Or, as they become more sophisticated, they may say that it's clearly stated in their Unique Value Proposition. Whatever they tell you, it's all just yada, a meaningless description that defines nothing yet allows business owners to present themselves as the best (as if five competing hamburger joints could possibly all really be "the best"). No matter how they describe their product or service, it's just ground round.

Let's stop considering any more of this yada and move on to some real-world techniques for providing customer service. What follows is based on 15 years of learning the hard way and continually testing new approaches to customer service. In my case, we call it client-centered service.

To supplement my philosophy that running a successful small business is about value and not price, there are two excellent sources worth mentioning. You should check them out. Sarah Petty and Erin Verbeck, in their book, "Worth Every Penny", offer a radically different way to run a small business, one that doesn't succumb to the pressure to discount prices but instead makes price irrelevant by creating a superior client experience. Visit them at www.joyofmarketing.com.

Also, John DiJulius' company, The DiJulius Group, has created an unusual strategy for business to boost their bottom line by focusing on – you guessed it – world class customer service, typically incomprehensible to most of the big boys. Read John's book, "What's The Secret?" or visit him at www.thedijuliusgroup.com.

Since all of us are somebody's clients, what might lead us to believe "they" (our actual clients), want something different from "us"?

The simplest way to describe client-centered service is to say that it's the same thing *we* want when *we* buy stuff – value.

Client-centered service is not price-driven. As a matter of fact, in 15 years, we have never lowered our prices. In our founding year, our per-man-hour rate was $50. It now averages over $100, and it's certainly not because of smoke and mirrors. We simply discovered that they, our clients, wanted the same thing we did – value. So, instead of mortgaging our homes for a third time in order to invest in a humungous pile of marketing books, we just looked inward.

## Value vs. price

Some of your clients shop at K-Mart, some at Williams-Sonoma. Some stay at Motel 6, some at the Ritz-Carlton. Some drink Two Buck Chuck, some Coppola. Some carry the American Express Platinum card, some cut up their credit cards. American culture is defined mostly by price. Do you know anyone who's not at least a little curious when they see "50% Off Everything in the Store?" Why?

In the wealthiest nation on earth, we're all looking for a deal. Remember those times when we pounced on that 50% off sale and then wondered why the sweater shrank or there was construction going on outside our bargain-priced motel room? Are we that stupid? Yup. But somewhere in this forest of bargain-basement prices, there's a guy who's had enough. He's ready to leave a world too often infiltrated with junk products and lousy service and squeeze that last elusive dollar from his already-tapped out bank account for one sweet breath of fresh air – something that's of real value.

Petty and Verbeck say "The Internet, big-box stores and low-price local stores don't make it impossible to compete in your marketplace, but they do make it impossible to compete on price. You can't and shouldn't pursue this strategy."

While clients appreciate value, they may also want you to lower your price. You can do so, but only after you've determined there will be no diminishment in the quality of your service. The integrity of your service builds the integrity of your company. Do the job right, no excuses.

Since every client should receive your Guarantee of Quality, you can't cut corners. Prepare a postcard-sized Guarantee of Quality handout that spells out your guarantee with five bullet points and give it to every client. You can't scrimp on value because value is the reason why your clients return to you time and again. It's this value that will keep your company growing and avert the need to compete with price-conscious low-ballers. It may take you awhile to get there, but don't give up value for just for a sip of Two Buck Chuck. You give value because you are valuable.

To reinforce the value of Value, you need to think about all those times you handed over your credit card hoping for something good in return. Maybe you made a monthly payment early to avoid the added interest but actually missed it by a day. Maybe you bought the extended one-year warranty to cover a product or service that ought to work for longer than 90 days, but then stopped working a year and a day later. Maybe your dentist won't charge you much more for all the work that's not covered by Delta Dental. Maybe.

Do you get a sense that we are treading on thin ice every time we take out our wallets? How often does it look like a "keep your fingers crossed" situation? How many times are you willing to get mildly poisoned and still return to the same well? Is this just the nature of things nowdays?

**Is this really customer service?**

You have countless examples of customer service available. From businesses in your local area to companies thousands of miles away, and even government institutions, every day you experience all manner of what passes for customer service. Here's an example.

*Paradigm Tree Service* – The liquidambar in your front yard hasn't been pruned in 15 years. It's late autumn and leaves are all over the place.

You have a vague recollection that you paid somebody a couple hundred bucks to prune it way back when. You thumb through the phone book and see a full-page ad for Paradigm – they give free estimates. They must be a successful tree service to have such a big ad, so you call them, and Larry, the owner, arrives within half an hour. Wow – these guys are good.

Larry says, "It looks like a $500 job to me." You're taken aback, so he changes course. "But I'm gonna be doing another job around the block tomorrow, so I'll do it for $300 cash." You think, "That's great – the price has only gone up a hundred bucks in 15 years." You say, "Where do I sign?" and he responds, "No problem, I'll see you tomorrow at eight."

His crew arrives the next day around noon, and within minutes, your liquidamber has been reduced to a skeleton of sawed-off sticks. He asks for the cash and tells you his boys will be back tomorrow to clean up the debris. You pay him, even though your tree looks like a scarecrow.

Three weeks later, early in the morning, you hear noises out front. There's two guys raking up the debris and stepping all over your plants. Is this really customer service?

This example illustrates one of the many instances of conditioned response that we take for granted because we can't do anything about it. When it comes to truly honoring our fellow human beings through work, we must reexamine this habit of conditioned response and push our real preference to the forefront. Our preference should be to offer value, not loss. But this habitual conditioning requires a jolt to get us out of bumper-to-bumper traffic and into the fast lane. In the movie Moonstruck, Loretta (Cher) is exasperated with her new love, Ronny Cammarari, and shouts, "Snap out of it!"

Let's look at how you and your clients can snap out of it.

### What is client-centered service?

At the heart of client-centered service is the proposition that there is an emotional motivator that continually unfolds during all sales transactions. These most basic human interactions are rarely understood by business owners as having much to do with providing real service. I believe this emotional element is the primary component that drives all of us to buy on not buy. Below are words from a few companies that actually get it.

### The Ritz-Carlton-ism
- "Anticipate and fulfill the unexpressed needs of our guests."

### Disney-ism
- "Creating magical moments."

### Starbucks-ism
- "We are not in the coffee business serving people; we are in the people business serving coffee."

These isms taken from John DiJulius' book illustrate what I call the "reverse effect," that is, taking the age-old sales approach and flipping it 180°. The old school has always assumed that we need to "sell" our customers on our products or services. But if you reverse the concept, you could say that your customers need to sell *you* on what it is *they* really want. When you give clients what they really want, great service, they keep coming back. You don't have to "sell" them anything.

Here are some ways you can set the emotional tone for a value experience:
- Greet your clients at the door.
- Find out what they really want on an emotional level.
- In the store, take them to the location of the product they want.
- On the job, call them ahead of time to let them know when you'll be there.
- Ask if they have a preference for when they'd like the work done.
- Help customers obtain the necessary paperwork, permits, licenses, etc.
- Consult with their neighbors to ensure that everyone is happy.
- Explain the methodology behind what you do.
- Give an immediate refund if there are any complaints or damage.

- Give or send them a copy of the paid invoice with an invitation to come back.
- Keep records to notify customers when future service is recommended.
- Feature photos of their jobs and recommendation letters on your website.
- Upon completion of the transaction, ask their opinion on how you did.

### New ways to market value

- Host an event.
- Be a guest speaker or conduct a workshop.
- Give special rewards to your best customers. (Use the Pareto Principle which states that 80% of your business comes from 20% of your customers.)
- Devise a realistic social media methodology. This is a tough one because it can't just be about selling; it must also address a service.
- Ask your customers what they would really *love* to have you do. This could bring some valuable ideas because you're looking for suggestions above and beyond the average service or product.

Because "price" is ingrained in all of us as the normal way we value things, we need to revisit the idea that customer service is ultimately more important than price. Take a moment to review the objectives of client-centered service.

### Objectives of client-centered service

- To fully understand and appreciate the concept of service.
- To create an emotional bond with your customers.
- To further develop new and better customer service.
- To ensure that clients continue to return to you regularly.
- To offer your clients services they can't get elsewhere.
- To show examples of poor service and contrast those examples with the kind of service you provide.

- To understand what initially drives buyers – price.
- To replace price with value as a motivator.
- To continually break new ground as a small business.

Janelle Barlow and Dianna Maul offer a valuable observation in their book, "Emotional Value: Creating Strong Bonds with Your Customers":

"• Only 14% of customers who switch providers do it because they were unhappy with the quality of the product; most make the move because they were dissatisfied with the service they received.
• Nearly 3/4 of all customer purchases are made by repeat purchasers.
• The cost of gaining a new customer is nearly five times that of keeping an existing client.
• The best service providers keep their customers nearly 50% longer than their competitors."

### How to give client-centered service

The number one preferred method for interacting with your clients is face-to-face meetings. I have yet to find anything that can replace one-on-one human interaction, not emails, not newsletters, not postcards, not newspaper ads, not anything that doesn't place you squarely in front of your client. Below are some ways you can further develop your client-centered service.

### Ask for ideas

Great ideas come from trying new things. To prove value over price, it takes a different mindset. Asking your clients for their ideas helps you develop new practices based on real-world interaction. The more you understand what motivates your clients, the more you can deliver exactly that. Tell your clients that you're continually developing new ways to help them; invite them to participate; and listen, because they'll tell you.

### Ensure that clients return

Why measure customer satisfaction? The less time you spend searching for new customers the more time you have for your loyal returning customers. John DiJulius offered some national statistics: Only 6% of shoppers who experienced a problem contacted the company about it, whereas 31% shared the problem with friends or colleagues. (Source: "The Retail Customer Dissatisfaction Study 2006 conducted by The Jay H. Baker Retailing Initiative at Wharton and the Verde Group of Toronto.) After you've finished the job or sold the product, call all of your clients back to find out what they thought.

### Offer them what they can't get elsewhere

Listen closely when your client tells you how unsatisfied they were with the last product or service they received. This will give you a clear picture of the kind of service to avoid at any cost. Look out for your client; become a member of their team as if it were your own. Be proud of your product or service on their behalf and always go one extra step beyond what any other company would do.

### Contrast poor service with your service

Instead of rattling off a long, boring, and totally predictable list of things that you do, surprise your client by telling them exactly what you won't do. Give them examples of the sloppy service your competitors provide. In all my born days, I've never found any excuse for lousy service, but it happens all the time. You're the pro. Once you've demonstrated how others fail to provide great service, give your client an opportunity to see your level of expertise.

### Let your competitors have it

To provide better service at a lower price is a fallacy. We've all been burned on that slippery slope. You get what you pay for, and thank God for that age-old wisdom; it proves true in nearly every purchase made. Occasionally, you'll get price shoppers who haven't been burned yet. These negotiators will push all your buttons except the right one – the value button. Ultimately, your expertise and confidence will help them make the right choice, or they may never call again. Either way, your value is undiminished so don't be troubled by losing a sale over price. That loss rightfully belongs to your competitors.

For emphasis, I'll borrow another comment from John DiJulius in the section of his book under the headline "Making Price Less Relevant." John is the owner of the John Robert's Spa, a chain of high-end salons. "More than 90% of our competitors are less expensive, in some cases considerably so, yet we are one of the busiest salons in Ohio while spending virtually nothing on advertising."

### The value test

In order to sell value over price, you must have some experience with it yourself. Take the value test to find out if you can command what you're really worth. Maybe "cheap" is the only approach you allow yourself to follow. Maybe you're really *not* worth it.

*Sometime in the last year you went to an expensive restaurant while on vacation or to celebrate a special event. Why did you do that?*

*Sometime in the last three years you bought an expensive computer, cell phone, or television when there were cheaper items available. Why did you do that?*

*Sometime in the last five years you bought a new refrigerator, washing machine, or dishwasher instead of searching the web for a used one. Why did you do that?*

*Sometime in the last ten years you bought a new car instead of a used one. Why did you do that?*

*Sometime in the last twenty years you bought a home instead of continuing to rent. Why did you do that?*

*Sometime in your life you bought something expensive even though your mind was shouting, "I can't afford it!"*

If you haven't done at least one of the above, you don't shop for value, you shop only for price. This is a red flag that indicates you will have a problem understanding how to get top dollar for the value of your products or services. If you don't think you're worth it, you're not.

That would be a shame because you offer more value than you believe and you're needlessly leaving money on the table every time you follow the lowball businesses down loser lane.

### Learn what is valuable to you

Make a list of businesses you use where you pay more than others charge for their products or services. Then ask yourself why you're willing to pay more. Your answers reveal why you're willing to substitute value for price. If you're confident that what you do for your clients no one else could do better, and you get a real sense of accomplishment at the completion of each job, you've replaced price with value. Now you and your clients are on the same team, working for the mutual benefit of each other.

This is true client-centered service. Even my dog, Jiggs, has demonstrated many times that a life of service is as rewarding for him as it is for me. Client-centered service places you at the center of your own motivation. It puts you in touch with yourself all day and gives value to what you call work.

This next interview is with a business that deals with both new and used equipment.

**Category: Sporting Goods**

Tom Frankl's primary offering at Play It Again Sports is new and used sporting goods followed closely by fitness and exercise equipment. He pays his customers on the spot for quality used equipment. If you trade in your gear for a new or used product, you'll get as much as 30% more than if you just take the cash. If you want to get top dollar for your equipment, Tom will even take it on consignment. Of course, you'll have to wait until it sells to collect.

*His team knows their equipment backwards and forwards; this is pro service for everything from baseball to football, golf, soccer, water sports, fitness and exercise. It's always nice to talk to an employee who knows as much or more than you do about your equipment. And this is a team who really cares about their customers, especially kids. Tom will also facilitate the donation of your equipment to charitable and non-profit organizations that benefit the community.*

Year started (or took over) the business: *1994*
Amount of startup capital (either a loan or your own money): *$250,000*
Obtained startup capital from: *Family*
Number of employees at startup: *4*   Number of employees today: *10*
Gross revenue first fiscal year: *n/a*   Gross revenue last fiscal year: *n/a*
How many years did it take before you started making a <u>satisfactory</u> profit: *6*

Most valuable idea or action you've taken: *Tom's immediate response without hesitation: Customer Service. They refer to it in their store as "Positively Outrageous."*

Least valuable idea or action you've taken: *At one point some years ago, Tom stopped advertising for several months. It didn't work out. Also, he never put much energy into selling online even though a number of associates had suggested that avenue as another potential revenue stream.* (Readers note: this is retail - see how important advertising can be for your business type?)

What's more important?

- The value of your services: _____    Or    - The price of your services: <u>X</u>

- Why? *Tom's customers come back often because, as he says, his products are "well priced."*

- Return customers: <u>X</u>        Or    - Advertising: _____

- Why? *Once you capture a customer and treat them right, they keep coming back.*

- Cash flow:  *X*        Or     - Credit rating: _____

- Why? *Tom doesn't want to rely on credit. He believes the business should support itself.*

- Understanding your financials _____ Or   - Being good at what you do: *X*

- Why? *If you're good at what you do, the financials will be good as well.*

Best advice for a new owner (or one who's not yet successful):

*Prepare to be physically at your business for at least the first five years. That means being there all the time so your customers get your personal touch and attention. Don't just rely on your employees; your customers need to see your passion. If you think you can own a business and not work in it, you're in for a shock.*

*Finally, be there even during the slow times because your customer list will eventually grow like a ball of yarn.*

Here are the highlights of Step Five for your quick review.

## CUSTOMER SERVICE HIGHLIGHTS

- It's not about price, it's about value.

- Don't assume you can give better service at a lower price.

- Prepare a postcard-sized Guarantee of Quality.

- The preferred interaction with your customers is face-to-face.

- Create an emotional bond with your customers.

## The Little Business Book Step Five – Customer Service

- Offer your customers what they can't get elsewhere.

- Contrast poor service with your service.

- Keep records to notify your customers of new products and services.

- Nurture return customers rather than just advertising for new ones.

- Take the value test to learn what is valuable to you.

## THE LITTLE BUSINESS BOOK SUMMARY

I hope you found The Little Business Book informative, inspirational, and entertaining. Follow the advice herein because it offers a realistic expectation of success. No matter what stage of business you're at, you'll never quite satisfy all of your aspirations. After 15 years in business, I thought I'd be able to say I'd seen everything and done everything, but there's always something that surprises me.

Here's a quick review of the five steps:

Administration – Establish a filing system that includes your billing and employee records. Hold regular meetings and keep them under an hour. Keep your licenses and certifications up to date and make sure you have adequate insurance.

Operations – Hire slowly and fire quickly. Prepare an employee handbook, give regular performance reviews, and hire an operations manager. Give your employees the proper training and safety guidelines. This will affect the cost of your Workers Compensation insurance and provide the highest level of customer service.

Finance – Set your revenue goals, hire a bookkeeper, and learn to read your Profit and Loss statement. Get good accounting software and do an annual budget. Review your cash flow regularly and keep your credit score up so you can get a loan.

Marketing & Sales – Use all of the Top Forty marketing tools that are listed with a star. Emphasize your high level of Trust, Credibility, Relationship, and Value. Listen to your clients and satisfy their requests and emotional needs.

Client-centered service – Customer service is the key to success. It's not about price; it's all about value. Give your customers the kind of value and service they can't get anywhere else. Your competitors may make a short-term gain, but you will be making a long-term profit.

Here are a few admonitions:

You could assume that you can run a successful business all by yourself; however, that would be foolhardy. You could pay your employees in cash under the table, but that might be illegal. You could go without Workers Compensation insurance; however, that could lead to a lawsuit. You could lowball your prices, but that might price you right out of business because price does not equal value.

You could claim great customer service, and that might force you to prove it. You could advertise only in the yellow pages, but there are more current methods. You could employ only cheap labor; however, you might get employees with no company loyalty, safety training, etc. You could disregard your customer's feelings, but that may close the door to any future business with them.

You could work nonstop 12-hour days, but you run the risk of burning out. Stress can kill you.

You have the power and ability to grow a successful business which will provide handsome returns. Work *on* your business as much as you work *in* your business and you will reach your goals or find even better ones. I can tell you that every day will yield a new learning experience but you give value because you are valuable. Expect unforeseen challenges and handle them with confidence.

After all your trials and tribulations have been hashed out, muddled through, pulled apart, and reassembled, step back for a moment, view the beauty of the world around you, and reflect on these words from a long-forgotten song:

"All of your life you believe that you're somebody else.
Someone you see every day in your dreams.
Now is the time to remember that it can be you playing the part, if you will only follow your heart."

Appendix

CASE STUDIES

## The Little Business Book Appendix

These case studies are a result of interviews I conducted with real businesses with annual revenues between $50,000 and $2 million. All have been through the fire and ice of small business ownership and each one has valuable advice to offer.

### Index of Case Studies

1. Contract Manufacturer ............................................................. 101
2. HVAC ...................................................................................... 103
3. Building Designer .................................................................. 105
4. Bakery & Deli ........................................................................ 108
5. Civil & Structural Engineer ................................................... 110
6. Chiropractor ........................................................................... 113
7. Funeral & Cremation Service ................................................ 115
8. Hair Salon .............................................................................. 117
9. Building Contractor ............................................................... 119
10. Small Business Service ......................................................... 121
11. Landscaping .......................................................................... 123
12. Auto Repair ........................................................................... 125
13. SBA Lender ........................................................................... 127
14. Business Consultant .............................................................. 130
15. Business Broker .................................................................... 134

The Little Business Book Appendix

**Category: Contract Manufacturer**

*Areias Systems delivers design engineering, manufacturing, and prototyping solutions to technology companies in the Silicon Valley. Clemm Noernberg, company founder has built a systematized operation, the administration of which could serve as the template for small businesses everywhere. Areias' metrics management and data records are at the core of Areias' administrative system and his design and engineering process has been the key to their success.*

Year started (or took over) the business: *1999*
Amount of startup capital (either a loan or your own money): *$2,000*
Obtained startup capital from: *Clemm used his own money*
Number of employees at startup: *1*   Number of employees today: *20*
Gross revenue first fiscal year: *$750,000*   Gross revenue last fiscal year: *$4.1 mil*
How many years did it take before you started making a <u>satisfactory</u> profit: *1*

Most valuable idea or action you've taken: *Organize and setup company processes and encourage everyone to use and improve those processes.*

Least valuable idea or action you've taken: *Not screening money-losing customers and orders more diligently.*

What's more important?

- The value of your services: <u>*X*</u>   Or   - The price of your services:_____

- Why? *Once customers start dealing with us, we get a lot of projects without any other competing bids.*

- Return customers:  _X_          Or    - Advertising: _____

- Why? *Quite simply, there are few extra marketing costs when you have return customers.*

- Cash flow:  _X_          Or    - Credit rating: _____

- Why? *Cash is king (but always have a credit line available and pay it back immediately).*

- Understanding your financials _____ Or  - Being good at what you do: _X_

- Why? *If you're good at what you do, you'll already understand your financials.*

Best advice for a new owner (or one who's not yet successful):

*Take care of good customers.*
*Most new customers come from word of mouth.*
*Get good accounting help.*
*Be extremely organized.*
*Do extensive cost analyses.*
*And finally, always show up to your appointments on time.*

The Little Business Book Appendix

**Category: Heating, Air Conditioning, and Architectural Sheet Metal**

# BOGNER SHEET METAL
## HEATING & AIR CONDITIONING

*This company had already been in business for three decades when Bob Ciapponi took the helm. Today, Bob specializes in heating and air conditioning installations for both residential and light commercial clients. Additionally, the company does general exhaust systems for restaurants, architectural sheet metal, and metal roofing. They provide ongoing service and maintenance for all of their specialties.*

Year started (or took over) the business: *1983*
Amount of startup capital (either a loan or your own money): *Monthly payments*
Obtained startup capital from: *Payment arrangement with previous owner*
Number of employees at startup: *10*   Number of employees today: *13*
Gross revenue first fiscal year: *$900,000*   Gross revenue last fiscal year: *$1.7 mil*
How many years did it take before you started making a satisfactory profit: *8-10*

Most valuable idea or action you've taken: *Purchasing the right kind of equipment to do the job effectively.*

Least valuable idea or action you've taken: *Not building the right kind of relationships with contractors.*

What's more important?

- The value of your services: _X_    Or    - The price of your services: _____

- Why? *Giving people what they really want is more important than what they pay for it.*

- Return customers: _X_         Or    - Advertising: _____

- Why? *Return customers will stay with you forever. That will lessen the need to do continual marketing for new prospects. These customers are your best source for referrals and advertising.*

- Cash flow: $\underline{X}$  Or  - Credit rating: _____

- Why? *It's so much easier to operate your business when you have the necessary cash available.*

- Understanding your financials _____ Or  - Being good at what you do: $\underline{X}$

- Why? *Your financials don't need constant review if you're good and know that you're making a profit. Your reputation of knowing that you're good and knowing what you're doing will grow your business.*

Best advice for a new owner (or one who's not yet successful):

*Three things: (a) Know what your pricing has to be in order to make a profit, (b) be profitable, and (c) pay yourself.*

The Little Business Book Appendix

**Category: Building Designer**

Building designers can come from a number of design-related backgrounds including people with degrees who aren't officially registered as architects. As is the case with most building designers, you need to be proficient with computer-aided design (CAD) systems to produce construction drawings. Nick Sinnott, the owner of Design Services specializes in design work for both commercial and residential structures as well as schools and medical buildings. He recently completed the design for an all-weather sports track at his local high school. Nick says that the bulk of his business nowadays comes from refurbishing existing buildings due in part to the recession, although new construction is beginning to pick up again.

Year started (or took over) the business: *2000*
Amount of startup capital (either a loan or your own money): *$8,000*
Obtained startup capital from: *His own money*
Number of employees at startup: *1*   Number of employees today: *1*
Gross revenue first fiscal year: *$35,000*   Gross revenue last fiscal year: *$12,000*
*(Nick's highest year gross was $50,000.)*
How many years did it take before you started making a satisfactory profit: *3*

Most valuable idea or action you've taken: *Establishing connections with networked similar businesses that link to additional work opportunities. It's also important to invest in the most current equipment.*

Least valuable idea or action you've taken: *Too much time working out of my geographic area and specialty.*

What's more important?

- The value of your services: _X_    Or   - The price of your services:\_\_\_\_\_

- Why? *Providing high value makes for satisfied customers that ultimately become return customers. If the value is there, the price will mirror that.*

- Return customers: _X_    Or   - Advertising: \_\_\_\_\_

- Why? *Return customers are a walking advertisement. Things go a lot smoother because we already have a history. In turn, that minimizes the number of questions and problems that may result from customers that are unaware of the process.*

- Cash flow: _X_    Or   - Credit rating: \_\_\_\_\_

- Why? *If you can maintain good cash flow, you'll have good credit.*

- Understanding your financials _X_    Or   - Being good at what you do: \_\_\_\_\_

- Why? *Assuming that you're good at what you do, you definitely need to understand your financials because if you don't, you can't see the whole picture.*

Best advice for a new owner (or one who's not yet successful):

*Focus on three things: (a) prompt performance, (b) good money management, and (c) quality of work and service to the client. Given that there are certain things not under your control, these are three things you can control.*

*Your customer is coming to you for your professional input. It's your job to educate them to the best of your ability.*

*Be cautious with partnerships, they don't always turn out well. Keep your priorities straight because the business will take all your energy and more. Plan for family and personal time.*

*When doing cost proposals, I offer a 1-hour free consultation so that I can determine the scope. Once you've determined the scope of work, if you're using the time and materials method, limit your price range to 25 percent low to high. Your top end estimated price should not be more than 25 percent greater than your base. If the scope is well-defined, I prefer to use a fixed amount for my services.*

The Little Business Book Appendix

Category: **Bakery and Deli**

It all began on Valentine's Day, 1978. When Gayle and Joe Ortiz installed their first Take a Number ticket dispenser, they had no idea it would spin thousands of times into the fabulous operation it is today. This medium-sized food service is a rosticceria (Italian deli with rotisserie), presenting handmade food with a café and espresso bar. Gayle's has shared the spotlight as Best Bakery so many times that the locals have lost track. Behind glass and under shiny lights, the classy displays feature pasta, salads, sandwiches and Joe's specialty, breads, legendary for their authenticity and flavor. This tasty delight factory goes through two tons of butter, one ton of chocolate, and thirty-six thousand eggs – every month!

Year started (or took over) the business: *1978*
Amount of startup capital (either a loan or your own money): *$20,000*
Obtained startup capital from: *Family members, banks, and their own savings*
Number of employees at startup: *1*   Number of employees today: *170*
Gross revenue first fiscal year: *$20,000*   Gross revenue last fiscal year: *N/A*
How many years did it take before you started making a satisfactory profit: *1*

Most valuable idea or action you've taken: *Giving our manager a percentage of the business and making her a partner.*

Least valuable idea or action you've taken: *Decisions we've made in dealing with different personalities e.g., employees and contractors.*

What's more important?

- The value of your services:  *X*    Or    - The price of your services:_____

- Why? *Without value, price means nothing. People will still come, even with higher prices, as long as they get value.*

- Return customers: <u>*X*</u>   Or   - Advertising: _____

- Why? *We no longer need to advertise as much as we used to, and when new customers arrive, they almost always become return customers.*

- Cash flow: <u>*X*</u>   Or   - Credit rating: _____

- Why? *We use a lot of raw materials and most vendors like payment within 10 days. We also have a huge payroll and we rarely use our line of credit, so cash is king.*

- Understanding your financials <u>*X*</u> Or  - Being good at what you do: _____

- Why? *You go into business because you love what you do, but you probably won't be doing that once you're up and running. You'll be doing everything else. Get to know the numbers.*

Best advice for a new owner (or one who's not yet successful):

*Quality and service are number one. You can't slack off on either of them. Understanding money and people management is also important; you should be checking your financials every month. When checking your inventories, break them down by type and percentage so you can see if costs are going up or down. And make sure you break your financials down by department and look at all the line items on your profit and loss statement as percentages.*

The Little Business Book Appendix

**Category: Civil and Structural Engineers**

In 1999, when Jon Ifland took over as President of the company his father founded thirty seven years earlier, the company had already been successful from its very inception. Though times had changed and Jon needed to ease the company into the 21$^{st}$ Century, he wasn't prepared for the impending doom that we now call the Great Recession of 2008. At present, Ifland Engineers provides design services for land and site developments, residential subdivisions, commercial, mixed use, and healthcare properties. They also do site preparation documents for site grading and drainage, utilities, sewer, and water use, as well as construction documents for contractors.

Year started (or took over) the business: *1962 – Jon, President 1999*
Amount of startup capital (either a loan or your own money): *$500 in 1962*
Obtained startup capital from: *Provided their own money*
Number of employees at startup: *3*   Number of employees today: *9 (23 before recession)*
Gross revenue first fiscal year: *$15,000*  Gross revenue last fiscal year: *$1.3 million (was $2.3 million before recession)*
How many years did it take before you started making a satisfactory profit: *3*

Most valuable idea or action you've taken: *Not being afraid to hire people smarter than me.*

Least valuable idea or action you've taken: *Not planning ahead. Because we didn't take the time to regularly formulate our future plans, it almost put us out of business. We never saw the train wreck (recession) coming.*

What's more important?

- The value of your services: <u>*X*</u>    Or    - The price of your services:_____

- Why? *A true measure of a good engineer is what value one adds to the project, such as designing a cost efficient plan, quickly getting plans approved by local governing bodies or being able to explain the steps of a project to a client in advance so they're prepared for what may come.*

- Return customers: *X*        Or    - Advertising: _____

- Why? *We don't sell a product that is widely needed by the masses because the average person doesn't undertake new or remodel construction projects every day. There is a high cost to acquiring new business, but it's not in advertising. Much of our business comes from repeat clients and referrals.*

- Cash flow: *X*        Or    - Credit rating: _____

- Why? *Cash flow pays the bills. Being able to obtain credit is irrelevant if you don't have adequate cash flow to pay down the debt.*

- Understanding your financials_____ Or - Being good at what you do: *X*

- Why? *If you're not good at what you do, financials are not going to matter because you likely won't have a successful business. But an owner needs to have someone in the business or a consultant who understands the financials and can explain the most critical points to the owner.*

Best advice for a new owner (or one who's not yet successful):

*Get your ego out of the way and hire people that are smarter than you. Then let them do what they do well. It's important that you get the right people onboard, and even more important that you get the wrong people out of your business as soon as possible.*

(Here's some notable backstory from Jon) *When things were really booming around 2005-2007, we got so immersed in the day-to-day of trying to keep up with the demand for our services that we failed to stop and look up to see the train wreck headed our way (the recession). By not seeing the signs that started formulating as early as 2006, we were caught off guard and forced into a reactive mode when the phones stopped ringing. As a result, we didn't cut expenses fast enough and that had almost catastrophic impacts on our cash flow.*

*Instead of making drastic cuts early, we ratcheted down the entire time our business was eroding. We were extremely lucky to survive that period. It was only due to the profitability of the firm in the years leading up to the recession and the massive financial sacrifices of the owners that we were able to weather that storm. But it was a very close call.*

Category: Chiropractor

## McNabb Chiropractic Clinic

*Greg N. McNabb, DC has been an active and very passionate Dr. of Chiropractic for over 30 years. He is considered a wellness expert specializing in natural holistic healthcare and state-of-the-art chiropractic to improve the quality of one's life.*

*Based on the prestigious Gonstead method of spinal analysis and correction, he is able to correct different kinds of neuromusculoskeletal disorders using specific painless, spinal adjustments.*

*When indicated, nutritional testing, dietary consultation, and nutritional protocols are prescribed to improve and support various functions of the body.*

*Dr. McNabb's typical interface with new patients includes: a consultation, physical examination, and lab tests and/or x-rays if necessary.*

Year started (or took over) the business: *1979*
Amount of startup capital (either a loan or your own money): *$20,000*
Obtained startup capital from: *Personal loan from a family member*
Number of employees at startup: *2*   Number of employees today: *2*
Gross revenue first fiscal year: *$95,000*   Gross revenue last fiscal year: *$250,000*
How many years did it take before you started making a satisfactory profit: *2*

Most valuable idea or action you've taken: *Learning patient management skills using effective communication because this is a people business.*

Least valuable idea or action you've taken: *Investing in market strategies that resulted in little or no return on investment.*

What's more important?

- The value of your services: _X_   Or   - The price of your services:_____

- Why? *In my opinion, chiropractic care and nutritional therapy are the most valuable aspects of achieving true health than any other types of care available.*

- Return customers: _X_   Or   - Advertising: _____

- Why? *Having return patients tells me that my message of natural health care is "getting through" to them and that it has made a difference in their lives. They understand that securing and maintaining health is a journey, not a destination.*

- Cash flow: _____   Or   - Credit rating: _X_

- Why? *A good credit rating is more important over the long haul.*

- Understanding your financials _____   Or   - Being good at what you do: _X_

- Why? *You can buy brains for financials, but you can't buy proficiency and appropriateness in your field.*

Best advice for a new owner (or one who's not yet successful):

*Know that competence in your field leads to a stronger belief in your service or product. Have a thorough understanding of effective marketing strategies to drive the public to your business. Place a great deal of emphasis on service. My father, who was a successful businessman and politician, always told me to give the people more than they expect.*

The Little Business Book Appendix

Category: Funeral & Cremation Service

When Gary Benito and Vince Azzaro took over this business, they had quite a hill to climb to get the place in shape. Nowdays, they are a full service funeral home whose services include burial cremation, the sale of merchandise associated with funerals and cremation, logistics, and planning a beautiful farewell ceremony.

Year started (or took over) the business: *2000*
Amount of startup capital (either a loan or your own money): *$400,000 in loans*
Obtained startup capital from: *Bank loan and also $400,000 of their own money*
Number of employees at startup: *5*   Number of employees today: *10*
Gross revenue first fiscal year: *$250,000*   Gross revenue last fiscal year: *2 million*
How many years did it take before you started making a satisfactory profit: *5*

Most valuable idea or action you've taken: *Took advantage of the opportunity to purchase a list of "pre-needs" customers from a local funeral service that had recently gone out of business. Present day funeral operations are different than they were a decade ago. Now, most pre-existing arrangements are done through burial insurance.*

Least valuable idea or action you've taken: *Both Gary and Vince's skill sets as funeral directors were fully up to speed when they took over the business, but they had little experience in working <u>on</u> the business as opposed to just working in the business. In other words, they were technically adept at their jobs, they just didn't know a lot about running a business.*

What's more important?

- The value of your services: <u>X</u>   Or   - The price of your services:_____

- Why? *Providing quality service rather than trying to compete on price allows us to give our customers the best, the most caring, and the most well-rounded service possible.*

- Return customers: <u>X</u>   Or   - Advertising: _____

- Why? *We spend more than we should on advertising. The emphasis has to be on our personal relationships, our brand of service.*

- Cash flow: <u>X</u>   Or   - Credit rating: _____

- Why? *Cash is the life blood of just about any business.*

- Understanding your financials _____ Or  - Being good at what you do: <u>X</u>

- Why? *If you're not good at what you do, you probably won't last very long.*

Best advice for a new owner (or one who's not yet successful):

*There has to be no limit to what you'll do to be successful. You have to be willing to do everything necessary. If not, you should probably work for someone else.*

The Little Business Book Appendix

Category: Hair Salon

Sally Spalding came up through the ranks as a hairstylist working for the prestigious Gene Juarez firm at a large metropolitan location in the Pacific Northwest. After moving to a smaller community, Sally started Salon Luxe, re-creating, at a boutique level, her years of experience with color, extensions, eyelashes, Brazilian blowouts, mani-pedis, balayage, highlighting, and waxing. Sally is the lead technician and hair dresser along with four other stylists. The other stylists each lease a chair. Husband Scott manages the financials and both of them manage their five kids ranging in age from one to eighteen. Who said running a small business is like a part-time job? I don't think so. But it pays off in more ways than one. In their first year, Salon Luxe was voted Best Salon, and Sally was voted Friendliest Beautician.

Year started (or took over) the business: *2013*
Amount of startup capital (either a loan or your own money): *$30,000*
Obtained startup capital from: *Loan from a relative*
Number of employees at startup: *4*   Number of employees today: *6*
Gross revenue first fiscal year: *$52,373* (Only in business one year to date as of this writing)
How many years did it take before you started making a satisfactory profit: *Not yet*

Most valuable idea or action you've taken: *Opening my business instead of working for another company. We lease our chairs to our stylists so we don't offer any salaries or benefits. The most important thing is that we provide them with the retail product and that's where we make our money.*

Least valuable idea or action you've taken: *At the company I used to work for, I was paid a minimal commission and the company made all the rest. Because we now lease our chairs instead of paying commissions, I may be missing out on additional revenue, but I prefer to do it that way. Our stylists like it, they're happy and they bring in consistent business.*

What's more important?

- The value of your services: *X*     Or     - The price of your services:_____

- Why? *My experience is more valuable because of my previous salon background and education.*

- Return customers: *X*     Or     - Advertising:_____

- Why? *In the hair dressing business, our biggest asset is referrals. 95% percent of our business comes from referrals.*

- Cash flow: *X*     Or     - Credit rating:_____

- Why? *We're not a big enough business to even worry about a credit rating or getting a loan.*

What's more important?

- Understanding your financials _____ Or   - Being good at what you do: *X*

- Why? *There would be no financials if I wasn't good at what I do. Besides, Scott handles all the financials.*

Best advice for a new owner (or one who's not yet successful):

*Get experience in your industry first. Understanding the ins and outs of your industry is of the utmost importance. Seeking the wisdom of those who came before and creating a solid foundation of knowledge and experience will start you out in the right direction. Start small and don't get financially strapped in the beginning.*

Category: **Building Contractor**

*In 2000, Sid Slatter and his brother, Matt took over the reins of a company started by their parents sixteen years earlier. The brothers have hands-on experience in many facets of the construction trade with particular emphasis on commercial, medical, hospital, grocery, and even residential though that's not a mainstay of their business. Not only are they licensed general building contractors, but they're also licensed engineers which brings them into projects involving private construction as well as bridges and retaining walls.*

Year started (or took over) the business: *2000*
Amount of startup capital (either a loan or your own money): *$10,000 in 1984*
Obtained startup capital from: *Their parents*
Number of employees at startup: *5*   Number of employees today: *25*
Gross revenue first fiscal year: *$250,000*   Gross revenue last fiscal year: *12 million*
How many years did it take before you started making a <u>satisfactory</u> profit: *5*

Most valuable idea or action you've taken: *When we reached the level of 100 employees, we decided it was too unwieldy so we switched over to using sub-contractors which cut our in-house payroll significantly. We also hired a full-time business development person to focus on bringing in work from other geographic areas.*

Least valuable idea or action you've taken: *Because we had enough space at our location and we were looking to expand the business, we decided to start up a full-time cabinet shop. We learned in short order that because it wasn't one of our specialties, it also wasn't really our cup of tea. Be careful what new things you think you should add to your business model.*

What's more important?

- The value of your services: _____    Or   - The price of your services: *X*

- Why? *We can't make it without getting the right price.*

- Return customers: *X*    Or   - Advertising: _____

- Why? *80% of our business is repeat customers.*

- Cash flow: *X*    Or   - Credit rating: _____

- Why? *If you can't pay your bills, you're in trouble.*

What's more important?

- Understanding your financials _____ Or  - Being good at what you do: *X*

- Why? *You can hire someone to work with your financials, but you must be really good at what you do.*

Best advice for a new owner (or one who's not yet successful):

*Start slow until you understand the flow. When you finally begin making money, hold on to some of it in anticipation of future events (like a recession).*

The Little Business Book Appendix

**Category: Small Business Service**

   *Terry Guy has been in the tax preparation business most of his life. He's always been self-employed and enjoys the challenge of the ever-changing tax codes. Over the years, the business has grown to include not only tax preparation for both individuals and businesses (corporations), but also Terry's company handles estate taxes, audits, entity formation and compliance, payroll, and business legal. Small Business Consulting, Inc. presently has over 800 individual clients and processes some 1,200 returns annually.*

Year started (or took over) the business: *1967*
Amount of startup capital (either a loan or your own money): *$500*
Obtained startup capital from: *Savings*
Number of employees at startup: *0*  Number of employees today: *6*
Gross revenue first fiscal year: *$20,000*  Gross revenue last fiscal year: *$735,200*
How many years did it take before you started making a <u>satisfactory</u> profit: *1*

Most valuable idea or action you've taken: *Bundling services and hiring experts for each area.*

Least valuable idea or action you've taken: *Trying to add HR (Human Resources) as another bundle.*

What's more important?

- The value of your services:  *X*  Or  - The price of your services: _____

- Why? *This is a very competitive business. You have to offer your clients a variety of services.*

- Return customers: _X_    Or    - Advertising: _____

- Why? *New startups take considerably more time. Once a client is up and running, we have a good handle on how to manage their continuing return business.*

- Cash flow: _X_    Or    - Credit rating: _____

- Why? *Terry is able to carry Accounts Receivable on his own and has excellent credit.*

- Understanding your financials _X_    Or    - Being good at what you do: _____

- Why? *We've developed our own software to monthly regulate the work flow and income derived from each employee.*

Best advice for a new owner (or one who's not yet successful):

*Grow slowly, ask for referrals, follow up on emails and phone calls daily, and turn work around in a reasonable time frame. Also, make sure you have enough cash available to take care of at least one month's worth of expenses.*

The Little Business Book Appendix

Category: **Landscaping**

*The creation and implementation of beautiful and romantic gardens is the primary reason Nikos Lynch established Terra Bella Landscaping. After winning numerous awards for his unique water features, lighting, xeriscape, and custom residential and commercial designs, Nikos adopted the tagline Gardens for a Lifetime, and they truly are. He utilizes low water use principles and adds such functional features as BBQ's and pergolas. By offering sustainable landscaping, Nikos' gardens create a world that his clients can enjoy for a lifetime.*

Year started (or took over) the business: *1996*
Amount of startup capital (either a loan or your own money): *$10,000*
Obtained startup capital from: *His own money*
Number of employees at startup: *3*   Number of employees today: *9*
Gross revenue first fiscal year: *$250,000*   Gross revenue last fiscal year: *$850,000*
How many years did it take before you started making a <u>satisfactory</u> profit: *3*

Most valuable idea or action you've taken: *Getting mentorship, having someone to get advice from.*

Least valuable idea or action you've taken: *Initially started as a partnership. When we realized we were working from two different check books, that's when it started to go downhill. After that I grew the business on my own.*

What's more important?

- The value of your services: <u>*X*</u>   Or   - The price of your services:\_\_\_\_

- Why? *Beautiful gardens are not only a home improvement, they can actually be a life enhancement offering a needed respite from the cares of the day.*

- Return customers: <u>*X*</u>     Or     - Advertising: _____

- Why? *Advertising is expensive and nothing is guaranteed with your layout of cash. Return customers bring you money.*

- Cash flow: <u>*X*</u>     Or     - Credit rating: _____

- Why? *With a loan, you become a slave to whomever you borrow money from, and ultimately you end up paying more in the long run.*

- Understanding your financials: <u>*40%*</u>  Or   - Being good at what you do: <u>*60%*</u>

- Why? This is a tough one to choose from, but you can always find talent who are good at being equally a technician and a tactician. When you're good at what you do, your reputation reflects that.

Best advice for a new owner (or one who's not yet successful):

Always make your bottom line. Beyond that, be innovative. Just about everyone can set their prices, but you need to time track to see where you're losing or making money.

Get involved with other people in your industry. This will make for some good collaboration and allow you to vet other businesses that you can recommend to your clients. By making these established connections, you can call them in when you need them.

Category: Auto Service & Repair

*Here's a company whose overall business philosophy matches mine. It's all about customer service. Ten years after Henry and Lisa Carter started Water Star Motors, they became the first Green-certified business in their town and it was only up from there. They've received numerous local and state awards for Best Small Business of the Year. In addition to auto repair, they're a Certified Smog and Repair Station. Henry is also a past President of the Exchange Club and Lisa is a past board member of the Exchange Club, The Sustainability Academy, and Next Stage Productions. Their personal philosophy is "Work Hard, Play Hard" which means they've visited such distant places as Machu Picchu along with their regular hangout, Cabo San Lucas in Mexico. Water Star Motors is the perfect example of a small business totally involved in their community*

Year started (or took over) the business: *1993*
Amount of startup capital (either a loan or your own money): *2 months free rent*
Obtained startup capital from: *had own tools valued at $100K*
Number of employees at startup: *2*   Number of employees today: *5*
Gross revenue first fiscal year: *$40,000*   Gross revenue last fiscal year: *$1 mil*
How many years did it take before you started making a satisfactory profit: *9*

Most valuable idea or action you've taken: *Hired a business consultant and became a member of the "Smart Group".*

Least valuable idea or action you've taken: *Tried doing a radio show, had fun with it, but it didn't bring in any notable revenue.*
What's more important?

# The Little Business Book Appendix

- The value of your services: <u>X</u>    Or    - The price of your services: _____

- Why? *Customers like a good experience and we are an experience-based business. We don't sell price. It's all about service.*

- Return customers: <u>X</u>    Or    - Advertising: _____

- Why? *Our best customers are the ones we have a relationship with, and our return customers spend more.*

- Cash flow: <u>X</u>    Or    - Credit rating: _____

- Why? *We have zero debt right now and also an excellent credit rating.*

- Understanding your financials <u>X</u>    Or    - Being good at what you do: _____

- Why? *Henry manages the business and has a thorough understanding of his financials. He believes in working "on" the business, rather than just in it.*

Best advice for a new owner (or one who's not yet successful):

*Pay attention to everything that's going on; learn how to hire the right people, understand fully how your business works by getting help from an outside consultant, have good communications with your partners, keep your debt as low as possible, and show up no matter what. Persevere.*

Category: SBA Loans

## Robert Porter, SBA Business Development Officer

I had a wonderful conversation with a banker today. I learned a lot about why banks do what they do; local banks that is. Bob Porter has been with a local bank in Northern California for the last five years specializing in SBA loans. He actually started in the banking business twenty-five years ago and really knows his stuff.

He told me a somewhat surprising story. While in the banking business, he founded, as a sideline, what became one of the world's largest indoor rock climbing facilities. Being in the loan business himself, his partners asked him to go out and find the money for the startup. After six banks declined his loan, he learned that you have to be tenacious, and when the seventh bank said "Yes", they were off and running (or rather climbing).

Local lenders rely to a considerable degree on common sense. It's not just all about numbers. Think about it; if someone came to you and asked if they could borrow $100,000, would you automatically write a check? Maybe if you had just won the lottery. Bob looks at things such as how much confidence you have in your enterprise. He'd rather hear someone say, "Look, I'm doing this with you or without you" rather than "Will you pleeze loan me the money?"

I strongly recommend you deal with a local bank whose home office is nearby. I'm no longer comfortable dealing with a big bank. I'd much rather deal with local bankers any day of the week; they're more friendly and real.

So let's get on to the questions. Bob gave a quick and easy answer to the first one.

Is it correct to say that the SBA doesn't supply the funds, but instead guarantees repayment of the loan to the participating lender in the event of the borrower's default? *Yes.*

Does the business have to be operating before it can apply for an SBA loan? *No. About 10% of the loans made are to new startups.*

Does it matter if the business is organized as a sole proprietor, partnership, or corporation? *No.*

Who signs for the loan? *The owners, depending on how they're legally organized. And they sign both jointly and severally, meaning that not only is the company obligated, but each owner is personally obligated as well.*

Does the applicant need to put his/her own money into the business? *You must put in no less than 20% of your own money.*

Can the borrower have co-signers? *Yes, but they don't use the term co-signers; rather they're called guarantors. Also, the guarantors may be asked to pledge real estate or some other form of collateral.*

What types of collateral will the borrower have to provide? *Business assets, pink slips on vehicles, and personal real estate, among others.*

How is the dollar amount of the loan determined? *There are a number of different ways. For example, if you're buying a business, the seller may be asked to carry at least 10% of the loan. The seller may also be required to stay involved with the business for a period of time. A lot of common sense and subjectivity goes into this decision.*

Typical loan term? *Buying a business – 10 years; Working capital – 7 years; New startups – 10 years; Real estate – 25 years*

Average amount of time to close the loan and get funded? *Typical for Bob is 45 to 60 days, though he's seen it take longer.*

Assuming the loan payments are timely and consistent, can the borrower go back at a later date for additional funds (e.g., line of credit, loan increase, etc.?) *Yes. The SBA lender considers what's best for the borrower.*

**Necessary documents needed for the average SBA loan:**

1. A completed loan application.
2. List of personal income and expenses for the last year.
3. Business income tax returns for the last three years.
4. Personal income tax returns for the last three years.
5. Profit and loss statement for the last three years. (no less than one year)
6. Balance Sheet. (not required, but would like to see it)
7. Personal bank statements for the last two months.
8. Business bank statements for the last two months
9. Resume (part of #1, the loan application)
10. Business or personal credit report – not always
11. Business Plan - Yes
12. Competitor data - (part of #1, the loan application) *Note: Lender may do a Google search for your marketplace*
13. How will the loan proceeds be used – They want to see this to the penny.
14. Other – Other income like rentals, will the borrowers spouse continue working elsewhere?

Additional important considerations:

Lenders aren't just interested in making money; they're looking at the best interest of the borrower. They don't want to see families go bankrupt. They know that oftentimes the buyer of a business is buying more of the past than the future. You must have no credit card debt and very few car loans.

**Category: Executive Advisor and Business Consultant**

## Flamepoint Strategies

Bill Ross is the owner of Flame Point Strategies. After a 25+ year career in high-tech sales, marketing, and executive management, Bill has spent the last 10 years as an advisor to owners of privately held businesses aiding them in developing strategic growth plans and improving operational aspects of their businesses.

1. What's the most notable thing a new startup doesn't know?
   *It's not just about being a technician. It's not just about working in your business, it's also about working on your business, being aware of all those things that technicians normally aren't aware of and understanding their value and necessity.*

   *Also, everything has a cost and it's not just what you think it costs. As an example, even though you may think you can't afford to hire someone to do specific functions, you are actually paying more in lost opportunity costs by not doing the things that will make your business successful.*

2. What's the most important concept a new startup needs to understand?
   *You need to learn how to tie all the pieces together. You can't just ride your technical know-how to success. Everything needs to work together.*

3. What items should a new startup place less emphasis on in the beginning? (in other words, how easy is it to get sidetracked into filling the salt shakers when you're the owner of the restaurant?)
   *Stop insisting, "I have to do this!" There are many tasks that can be outsourced. To follow the example cited in the question, if you are filling the salt shakers, then you won't be spending the necessary time observing that your prospective customers are leaving because the waiting line is too long. More importantly, if you don't observe the issue, you won't understand why your*

*business is suffering and you won't be able to correct it. Most of the time, the business owner will end up doing things counterproductive to solving the problem (i.e., offering a discount to get more customers).*

4. What are some of the direct benefits a business can derive from using a consultant?
   *Consistent review, weekly, monthly, and annually. You get better bottom line results with an outside perspective that's not emotionally tied to your business. You also get different perspective and gain insight into business challenges and assistance in developing strategies to correct the issues.*

5. How does a business get new customers? What works more, what works less?
   *This is the age old challenge that most people think there is a magic answer to. If I advertise here or do a good job there, prospects will flock to my business. I call this the "Field of Dreams" syndrome. What you have to understand is that business is a process, a series of systems in play. You have to develop an actual Customer Acquisition Process, a written methodology. You also need to understand that there are two processes in play; one to produce prospects (those interested in your product or service) and one to convert them to customers. Develop your strategies, then follow through and actually implement them. There is no magic answer. What works for someone else may or may not work for you depending on a number of factors.*

6. Is there a preferred method for measuring an employee's value (e.g., paycheck)?
   *Much like the value of a business is measured by what it produces (profits), the value of an employee is measured by what they contribute to the whole. One needs to determine the direct (position) and indirect (team) metrics that will be used to judge an employee's contribution. One note: you need to share the metrics with the individual and the team and then review progress frequently. People need to know how they are being judged and how they are doing. Again, without a good group of employees*

*working together toward common goals, the results of the business will be severely handicapped.*

7. Reasons why a business might prepare an exit strategy (other than for exiting)?
   *If you don't know where you're going, how are you going to get there? You need to follow a path, have a plan to get things done.*

8. Committing things to paper – what kind of records/data/metrics contribute substantially to:

    a. Sales and Marketing
    *Once you develop your process, you should record, analyze and review the numbers at each step along the way. You need to keep track of what you invest (direct dollars, time, etc.) and what your return is. Let's suppose you are sending out marketing mailers. You need to record: how many sent, to what audience, what each cost, total cost (including labor time and money) and then the response rate. You also need to record how many of those that responded converted into customers. By doing so, you will be able to judge the effectiveness of the campaign and make a decision as to whether or not it is worthwhile repeating.*

    b. Cost management
    *While controlling costs is an important aspect of business success (and one you should be conscious of), I've never seen anyone cost-cut themselves into prosperity. You will find a much greater return if you spend your time and energy focusing on improving those items above the gross margin line.*

9. Employers are always trying to predict what their employees want. What do you think they want?
   *By and large, they just want a paycheck. Successful business owners are those that hire the right employees who will motivate themselves beyond just the paycheck.*

10. Is there any reason that a company's name, logo, or website could be as effective, maybe even more effective, than what the company actually does? (This is a small business vs. big business issue)
    *You need a presence, but too much concentration on logo, web, etc., doesn't work for small business. Let the big companies spend the heavy dough.*

11. If you're not producing enough revenue, where can you get it?
    *Look to your customers. They already know your business and have shown that they enjoy doing business with you.*

12. What's a likely outcome of not having specific sales goals?
    *No sales and thus no business. You've got to be committed on this one. Put it down on paper and follow it religiously.*

13. We all know what bad service is, but can you encapsulate what the average customer considers good service?
    *The bar has been lowered so much that bad or mediocre service can look like good service. Imagine your customer's response if you actually gave them really good service. It really comes down to putting your customers' best interests ahead of yours.*

The Little Business Book Appendix

Category: Business Broker

## Business Team, Inc.

Selling a business presents challenges. As founder and President of Business Team, Inc., Ian MacLachlan has seen his share of challenges since their startup in 1981. First and most obvious, how do you establish a price? Price too low, leave money on the table, price too high, nothing happens. Ian's company, with ten offices in the Western United States, is a matchmaker for small businesses valued up to $100 million. He's encountered just about every type of small business owner, some of whom think their business is worth much more than it really is.

When it's time to reap the rewards of all your years of effort devoted to nurturing your small or mid-size business, a little advance planning can pay off handsomely. Ian's company has sold over 4,000 businesses: high tech, low tech, manufacturing, service, retail, food and beverage, and just about every other type of business. When we sat down for this interview, it became quickly apparent that there's much more that goes into the process than meets the eye. Here are some of the questions I had for Ian:

Since all businesses are valued differently, what's the most common formula used to determine business value?

*Use a multiple of adjusted cash flow. Multiples can range from 2X to 5X, depending on the type of business. For example, if your adjusted cash flow is $200,000, then 2 X $200,000 means you should be able to list your business for $400,000.* [WEB SEARCH: Valuation using multiples]

*Adjusted cash flow is a business's earnings after expenses, but before interest, depreciation and taxes. It's sometimes referred to as Sellers Discretionary Earnings (SDE). You may also have to add or subtract your salary to arrive at your real net income. If this sounds complicated to you, it is. That's why I said there's more to business valuation than meets the eye.*

Subject to the type of business, what are some other methods used to determine value?

*There are many other methods, e.g., depreciated replacement cost, or percentage of annual sales, but the most predominant method is a multiple of adjusted cash flow.*

What role does goodwill play in determining value?

*I hate to break the news, but goodwill usually doesn't play much of a role in determining value. I know you've been in the same location for over twenty years and your customers all love you, but it almost always comes down to the numbers.*

Do web reviews like Yelp or customer testimonials or existing customer lists play a role in value?

*Only indirectly, but good reviews certainly can't hurt.*

Is there anything besides financials that can play a role in valuation?

*Lifestyle. For example, a motorcycle fanatic might want to buy a motorcycle dealership. Ian's company uses a rating system for all the other items that could create value.*

Is it easier to sell a sole proprietorship, a partnership, or a corporation?

*It doesn't matter how you're legally organized.*

Who signs the listing agreement with the broker?

*It depends on who the owner is. If you're a small corporation, you have to have authority from your shareholders which, in many cases, are the owners themselves.*

How long does a typical listing run?

*12 months.*

Is there a customary commission percentage (or flat dollar fee) paid to the broker and who pays it, the buyer or the seller?

*The seller pays the commission which is calculated as follows: minimum fee $15,000, followed by a sliding scale that ranges from 10 percent to 12 percent which could decline if the selling price exceeds $1 million.*

What's the average time it takes to sell a business?

*8 months.*

What are the typical services the broker will provide to a seller?

*The initial consulting process will arrive at the selling price, followed by a review of the marketing package. Then due diligence begins with the collection of all the necessary data. A cash flow analysis is done and the seller is coached on what to expect. Business Team provides confidential access to a large market of potential buyers as well as web exposure. When a buyer is found, a deal is negotiated and if the offer is accepted, the process is finalized with all the necessary documents going through escrow.*

What are the typical services the broker will provide to a buyer?

*Business Team can help arrange financing and, after consulting with the buyer, they will learn how much money the buyer has, how much management experience, and what the buyer's wish list is. Then the matchmaking begins.*

What types of documentation are required to do a business valuation?

1. *Business income tax returns for the last 3 years.*
2. *Profit and Loss statement for the last year to date.*
3. *Balance sheet.*
4. *Sales/marketing plan – could be a plus.*
5. *Operating handbooks – could be a plus.*
6. *Terms of lease.*
7. *Detailed disclosures are needed from both buyer and seller.*

# Glossary

Accrual Basis – One of several accounting methods accepted by the IRS for determining income taxes. On your Profit & Loss statement, you will record your income in the month that your customer signs the agreement (even though you may not provide the product or service in that month or collect the payment in that month). The same thing applies to payment of your expenses; you record the payment in the month that you incur the bill, even though you might not actually pay the bill until sometime in the future.

Balance Sheet – The balance sheet can be found on your accounting software and is used to determine all of your company's assets such as equipment and real estate. It also lists all of your liabilities such as loans and credit cards. If you have partners, it will list each partner's equity in your company. The balance sheet is always calculated for a particular point in time, such as December 31.

Cash Basis – The second type of accounting method accepted by the IRS for determining income taxes. On your Profit & Loss statement, you will record your income in the month that you receive it and your expenses in the month that you pay your bills.

Cash Flow – Since you need money in the bank to pay your bills, you have to know how much cash is available on any given day. You can prepare your own daily cash flow statement using an Excel spreadsheet (see Excel in this glossary). Using this spreadsheet, you can track how much money you will pay out today and how much you will take in. If you regularly have excess cash in your bank account, you may be able to do this weekly rather than daily.

(The) Cloud – You can use the cloud as backup storage for your computer. Cloud storage resides on an external server maintained by companies such as Microsoft, Carbonite, Dropbox, and Amazon that automatically back up and store data from your computer for quick and easy retrieval. In the event your computer crashes, you can access your backed-up files on the cloud from anywhere, on any computer, even your smartphone.

The Little Business Book Glossary

Demographics – Potential customers that fall within a specific age range.

Excel – This is software from Microsoft that is included with a half dozen other programs in Microsoft Office. Excel allows you to enter numbers in boxes (cells) and put the boxes in columns for mathematical calculations. You can use formulas that will calculate just about anything; for example, how much do you spend in an average month? You can also create pie charts and tables. The Microsoft Office package includes Word which is used for creating letters. Word allows you to drop in your logo at the top of the page, automatically check your spelling, and place photos in your document.

General Liability Insurance – Liability insurance protects you and your company from various claims for property damage, personal injury, and other damages that may occur in the operation of your business.

LLC – This is another variation of the many ways to legally form your company. An LLC (Limited Liability Company) is a hybrid that provides the limited liability of a corporation and the pass-through taxation benefits of a partnership. Ask your attorney and your accountant about the benefits of forming your company as an LLC.

Net Profit – The "bottom line", this is what you make after you pay all your bills. It can be used to determine the value of your company.

OSHA – The Occupational Safety and Health Administration is a federal agency with offices in most states that monitor safety in the workplace. As an employer, you must meet all the regulations established by OSHA. You are subject to periodic inspections and can be fined for safety violations. You should also be familiar with your own state's Department of Labor requirements.

Partnership – A partnership, as opposed to sole ownership, is a company that is owned by more than one person. Partners may be actively involved in the business or just investors. An attorney should prepare your partnership agreement and you should ask your accountant what accounting method you should use to pay your income taxes.

Profit & Loss Statement (P&L) – This is a financial statement that is prepared using your accounting software. It's also known as an income statement. The statement lists your total income for the period (one month, etc.), the total cost to provide your product or service for that period, and all other expenses such as rent, telephone, etc. for that period. After all these items have been deducted from your total income, what is left (the bottom line) is your net profit. I suggest you review your P&L statement monthly, but you can also prepare quarterly and annual statements. You can use this statement to determine whether you need to raise your prices or lower your expenses. Lenders typically require a copy of your most recent P&L.

Qualify – Qualifying is part of the sales process. It means determining, by various observations, whether the customer you are working with may become a buyer of your product or service. Qualifying your customer during your sales presentation will tell you if they are only interested in getting the lowest price or if they can really appreciate the value of what you are offering and are willing to pay for it. Qualifying tells you if your buyer is just looking, if they need to get someone else's permission first, or if your product or service will fully satisfy their need. Ultimately, qualifying informs you as to your customer's real motivation and keeps you from spending unnecessary time with someone who never intended to buy from you in the first place.

S-Corp – You can form your company as an S-Corp which is a legal entity similar to a partnership. This type of corporation may provide you with additional protection from liability, although that protection has been often challenged in the courts. Get a full explanation of the benefits of an S-Corp from your attorney and your accountant.

Workers Compensation Insurance – This is mandatory insurance that you must provide to each of your employees. It gives them medical care and some wage replacement in the event they are injured on the job.

## Bibliography and Recommended Reading

Attard, Janet. *Small Business Annual 2012 Chart*, © 2012 Attard Communications, Inc. Reprinted with permission from http://www.businessknowhow.com

Barlow, Janelle, and Dianna Maul. *Emotional Value: Creating Strong Bonds with Your Customers*. San Francisco: Berrett-Koehler, 2000. Print.

DiJulius, John R. *What's the Secret?: To Providing a World-class Customer Experience*. (Hoboken, NJ: Wiley, 2008). Print. Copyright © 2008 by John R. DiJulius III. All rights reserved.

Petty, Sarah, and Erin Verbeck. *Worth Every Penny: Build a Business That Thrills Your Customers and Still Charge What You're Worth*. (Austin, TX: Greenleaf Book Group, 2012). Print.

Wicks, Diana. *The Most Important Financial Report for a Small Business*. Demand Media. Reprinted with permission from http://www.demandmedia.com.

ACKNOWLEDGEMENTS

You can't make it in a small business as long as I have without the help and loyalty of your customers and employees, so they're the first on my list of thank-you's. Without them, there would be no story to tell. My wife and partner, MiMi, and our business partners, Amy and Jeremy Nama have been together in the trenches since the founding of our company 15 years ago. Without them, there's no story either. Our business adviser, Bill Ross has watched us go up and down like a yo-yo over the years. I expect he's nearly as exhausted as we are from dealing with the inevitable and sometimes daily changes that seem to fall from heaven (or hell, depending on your point of view).

To the participants in the case studies, all twenty of them, I say major thank-you's for their wisdom and insight: Scott Edelstein, Clemm Noernberg, Bob Ciapponi, Mike Wiechmann, Nick Sinnott, Gayle and Joe Ortiz, Dr. Anthony Giannotti, Jon Ifland, Andrew Townsend, Dr. Greg McNabb, Gary Benito and Vince Azzaro, Tom Frankl, Sally and Scott Spalding, Sid Slatter, Terry Guy, Nikos Lynch, Henry and Lisa Carter, Robert Porter, Bill Ross, and Ian MacLachlan.

Kathy Greenwood's bookkeeping advice was excellent, and how could I have stumbled through these pages without the kenai of my copy editor, Carolyn Woolston? Then there's my niece, photographer Dina Scoppettone Viara – great photo shoot! Thanks also to my accountant, Terry Guy, for his prudent counseling and tax preparation, and to my bookkeeper, Lara Carney, for her weekly updating of the financials. To Care'n King, my office manager, kudos for keeping my blood pressure below 130.

Finally, to every one of my customers, thanks for your loyalty. I'd list all of you, but there are over 6,000 customers in our database. What a journey! I need a cappuccino just to catch my breath. Rewarding, discouraging, creative, exasperating; I can handle those one at a time, but all at the same time? Phew, what an adventure.

## About the Author

The author with his granddaughters, Lily and Gia.

As the CEO of a successful small business for fifteen years, Dick Scoppettone has run the gauntlet from making payroll to making profit. Among his various passions over the years: songwriter, novelist, screenwriter, and web designer. Early on, he did a stint in show biz; nowdays it's all about small biz. For those who remember the Beatles era, Dick was the founder and lead singer of Harpers Bizarre, the pop group whose hit record *Feelin' Groovy* topped the charts in the Swingin' Sixties. He and his wife, MiMi make their home in Northern California.

## FUTURE BOOKS IN THE LITTLE BIZ SERIES

Learn how to run your own successful small business and interact with related businesses in your industry group.

Get in-depth information for each type of business listed below and how they work with other similar businesses in their group.

### THE LITTLE BUSINESS BOOK
For
E-Commerce
eBay
Craigslist

### THE LITTLE BUSINESS BOOK
For
Restaurants
Bakeries
Sports Bars

### THE LITTLE BUSINESS BOOK
For
Landscapers
Tree Services
Nurseries

### THE LITTLE BUSINESS BOOK
For
Auto Mechanics
Body Shops
Auto Parts

### THE LITTLE BUSINESS BOOK
For
Contractors
Building Designers
Civil Engineers

www.ingramcontent.com/pod-product-compliance
Lightning Source LLC
Chambersburg PA
CBHW051921170526
45168CB00001B/484